EASY CRAFTS for KIDS

Reader's
Digest
Children's Books®

Pleasantville, New York • Montréal, Québec • Bath, United Kingdom

Parent Letter

Easy Crafts for Kids is a child's passport to scores of fun and unique crafts. Each section has its own special theme that includes a wide variety of projects. Children will discover crafts to give as gifts and to decorate their worlds, while enjoying the interesting facts and helpful tips that accompany the projects.

Each page contains a list of materials needed for each craft. The materials should be gathered before doing the craft so you know what is needed and when to help your children. Some of the crafts include the use of art knives or scissors or the aid of an oven. Crafts that call for these tools should only be done with adult supervision, which is indicated throughout this book by this ✓ symbol.

On page 4, you will find a list of materials found in many of the crafts. For safety or convenience, consider substituting materials when possible. Many of the crafts include household items on the list of materials. You and your child can also keep an eye out for other things that can accomplish the same goals. This is a great way to recycle and also to promote creativity.

Remember, children should be encouraged to explore their own imaginations and not be restricted by any designs or colors suggested in the crafts. There is much to discover in **Easy Crafts for Kids**—enjoy!

CONTENTS

BASIC MATERIALS

- Black marker
- Colored markers
- Construction paper
- Crayons
- Googly eyes
- Paints: acrylic, poster, watercolor
- Paintbrushes
- Pencil
- Pipe cleaners
- Ruler

- Scissors
- Self-hardening modeling clay
- Stapler
- Tape
- Thread
- White glue
- White paper
- Cardboard
- Magazines
- Newspapers

ANIMAL CRAFTS

ANIMAL CRAFTS

Cartoon Animals

With some bristol board and a few paper fasteners, you can make animals that dance, run or flap their wings, just like in cartoons!

MATERIALS

- Bristol board
- Colored markers
- Scissors
- Round head paper fasteners

1

Using our model as a guide, draw the crocodile's body, legs and lower jaw on bristol board.

2

Color the crocodile with markers.

3

Cut out the legs. Attach them to the body with paper fasteners.

4

Cut out the crocodile's lower jaw and attach it the same way.

Try making other animals, like a dog, a duck or a chicken!

Talking Animals

Start with a paper fortune-teller and turn it into a talking animal!

HINT
When you fold, press edges firmly and run your fingers along the creases several times.

1

To make a frog, cut an 8-inch square of green construction paper. Fold it in half to make a triangle, and in half again to make another triangle. Unfold it completely.

2

Bring the four corners to the center and fold them in place. Turn the sheet over.

3

Bring the four corners to the center again. Fold in place. Fold in half to make a rectangle. Fold in half again to make a square. Unfold it back to a rectangle.

4

Slide your thumbs and index fingers into the four pockets so you can open and close the fortune-teller.

5

Cut eyes out of white paper and spots out of yellow paper. Glue them on and draw the rest of the eyes in black marker.

6

Cut a tongue out of red construction paper, 1 $\frac{1}{2}$ inches wide by 4 inches long. Draw a line down the center in black marker. Roll the tongue around a pencil to make it curl. Glue it inside the mouth. Your frog is ready to talk!

Papier-Mâché Creatures

Make your own giant dinosaur... or not so cuddly fish!

The papier-mâché technique involves wetting strips of newspaper with glue and then layering them to make a figure. The secret to success is in the drying. Be patient and let each layer dry well. Otherwise your figure may fall apart! Papier-mâché is a fun way to learn about sculpting.

MATERIALS

- 2 toilet paper rolls
- Balloon
- Masking tape, glue
- Newspaper
- Glue solution
- Poster paint
- Googly eyes

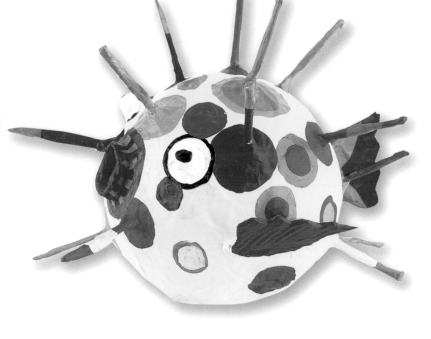

GLUE SOLUTION
You can make glue solution by combining four parts white glue and one part water.

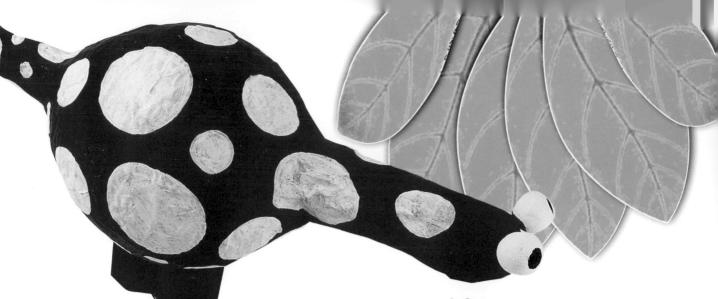

1

Inflate the balloon and tie a knot at the end. Cut the toilet paper rolls in half.

2

Stuff three rolls with newspaper. Tape two onto the balloon for feet. Tape one onto the front for the neck. Roll up a bit of newspaper for a tail and tape it onto the back.

3

Leave some newspaper sticking out of the toilet paper tube neck to help you form the head. Dip strips of newspaper in glue solution. Start wrapping them around the dinosaur's body.

To make the spikes on this fish, cover a few straws with papier-mâché and attach them to the body.

4

Cover the dinosaur completely in a layer of newspaper dipped in the paste. You will need to apply several layers, but you must let each layer dry thoroughly before applying the next.

5

When the last layer is dry, apply an undercoat of thick white paint, let it dry, and then paint a colorful pattern on your dinosaur.

6

Glue on the googly eyes.

Animal Streamers

Hang these streamers in your room and watch the animals turn slowly.

1 Draw your animals and the cheese on colored paper.

MATERIALS

- Pink, gray, yellow, brown and white paper
- Pink yarn
- Scissors
- Pencil
- Black marker
- Glue

2 Cut out the pieces and glue them together.

3 Add details with the black marker.

4

Glue your animals and cheese on long strands of pink yarn. Remember to leave some space in between them. Hang them from a light fixture or the ceiling, where they will slowly turn in the air.

You can use the templates below as a guide. When you are done, try making other streamers with other animals, like the sheep and elephant.

Animal Boxes

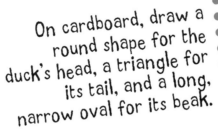

MATERIALS

- Cardboard box (from a computer or sound system, for example)
- Strong glue
- Pencil
- Black marker
- Acrylic paints
- Paintbrushes
- Foam paint roller
- Scissors
- Box cutter or art knife

The duck and the lion are ready for fun and adventure!

1

On cardboard, draw a round shape for the duck's head, a triangle for its tail, and a long, narrow oval for its beak.

head

2

beak

Cut out the pieces. Fold the beak twice, leaving a 1-inch band in the middle.

HINT
If you'd like, you can follow the same basic steps to make the lion shown here.

3

Glue the head and tail to the box. Glue the middle band of the beak to the head that's already been glued to the box.

4

Paint the duck white. Allow it to dry.

5

Paint the outline of the duck, the wings and the feet black.

6

Paint the rest of the duck red, yellow, white and black as shown.

Hand Animals

Paint a funny animal on your hand and watch it come to life when you move your fingers! Make a bunch of animals with your friends and you can put on a show!

MATERIALS

- Face-painting crayons or face paint
- Sponge
- Wide and fine paintbrushes

Crocodile

1

Put your hand in the position shown, outline the shape with black face paint and paint it in green.

2

Give it a second coat.

3

Paint the eyes white.

4

Use the black crayon to draw the teeth and the pupils of the eyes.

Monkey

1

Paint green stripes on your palm.

2

Paint red stripes in between the green ones. Paint the three middle fingers brown, as well as the tips of the thumb and little finger.

3

Paint the back of the middle finger yellow. Let dry. Paint the face of the monkey with black paint and a fine brush.

Parachuting Insects

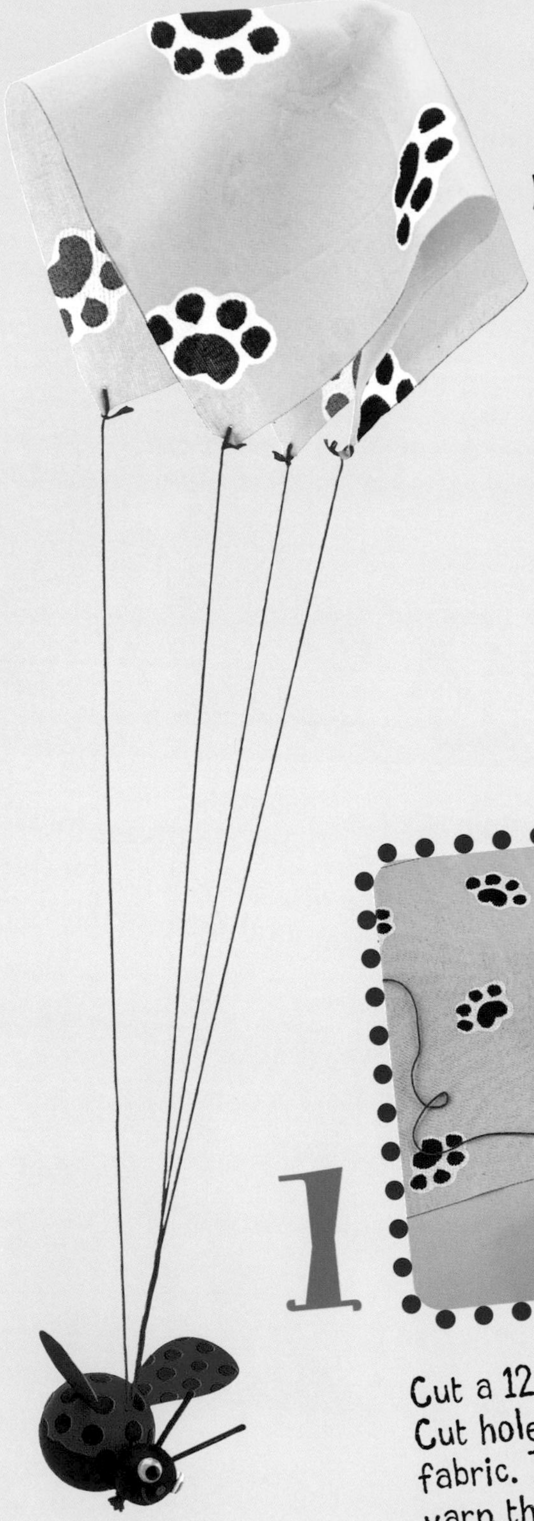

Have a parachute race for insects with your friends. Climb up somewhere and toss the bee and ladybug into the air. See who flies the fastest or farthest!

MATERIALS

- Lightweight fabric
- Four 12-inch pieces of yarn
- White construction paper
- Styrofoam balls (1-inch and 2-inch diameter)
- Pencil
- Acrylic paint and brushes
- Scissors and art knife
- Wooden skewer
- Toothpicks
- Googly eyes

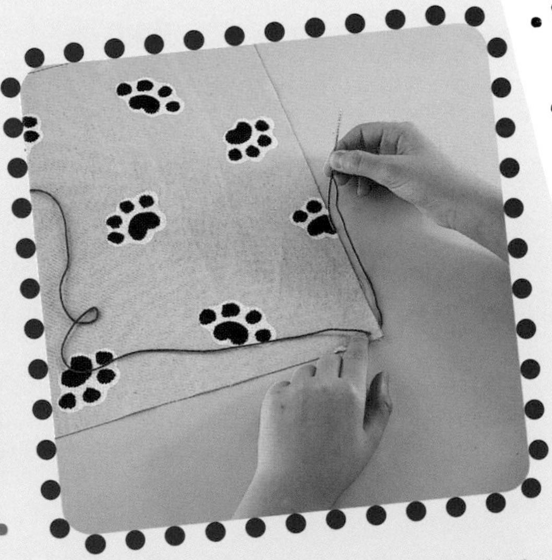

1

Cut a 12-inch square of fabric. Cut holes in the corners, of the fabric. Thread a piece of the yarn through the each of the holes and make a knot.

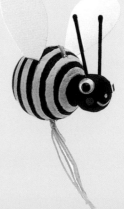

2

Draw two wings on the construction paper and cut them out.

Paint the body and wings in red and black or yellow and black as shown. Paint the head and two toothpicks black.

3

4 Pierce the body with the wooden skewer. Thread the four pieces of yarn through the hole and tie them in a knot to hold them in place.

5 Insert the toothpicks into the head and glue on the eyes. Insert another toothpick into the head and body to join them together. Make two slits in the body and insert the wings.

MATERIALS

- Styrofoam balls in different sizes
- Wooden skewers
- Yellow, red, black and white construction paper
- Acrylic paint and paintbrushes
- Glue
- Scissors and art knife
- Pipe cleaners

Spotted red or spotted black, these two cute characters are easy to make out of Styrofoam balls and construction paper. Just follow the instructions carefully.

1 Cut two medium Styrofoam balls in two for the feet.

2 Paint the head yellow, the body yellow and red, and the nose, horns and feet red. Paint the wooden skewers yellow and red as shown.

3 Glue on the nose and eyes. Paint the pupils black. Use short bits of skewer for the horns and tail. Stick two small red balls onto the horns.

4 Glue bits of pipe cleaner to the tail and head. Cut ears out of yellow construction paper. Cut two slits in the head and insert the ears.

Draw an oval on red construction paper for the body. Cut it out.

Cut half an oval out of black construction paper for the head. Glue it on to the body.

Cut four slits in the body as shown. Fold them inward so they overlap slightly and tape them together.

Cut the eyes, nose, antennae, legs and spots out of colored construction paper as shown. Glue them on.

Stick a wooden skewer through a small Styrofoam ball and pass it through the sides of the ladybug to make it roll!

Dancing Animals

A few small boxes, some corrugated cardboard and a little wire are all you need to make animals that dance in their own box!

1
Draw the separate parts of the animal on cardboard.

2
Cut out the parts.

MATERIALS

- Small cardboard box
- Corrugated cardboard
- Thin wire
- Scissors
- Glue
- Paint and brushes

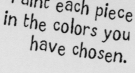

3 Paint each piece in the colors you have chosen.

4 Assemble your animal by attaching the pieces together with twisted wire.

5 Paint the inside and outside of the box.

6 Attach twisted wires to the head and back of your animal. Suspend it from the box by passing the wires through the top and side. Use the photos as guides.

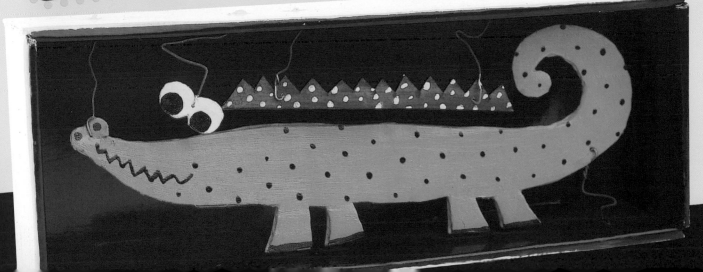

Paper Whale

Made of paper and cardboard, this whale rides over the waves and is ready to perch in a flowerpot or any other solid base.

1

Draw the whale on the cardboard and cut it out.

2

Tear strips of newspaper or magazine and glue them onto the whale.

MATERIALS

- Corrugated cardboard
- Magazines or newspapers
- Glue
- Paintbrushes
- Blue and white poster paint
- Scissors
- Wooden Skewer
- Empty tissue box
- Sand

3

Let it dry well. Give it an undercoat of white paint, and then paint blue over it.

4

Paint the facial tissue box blue, let dry, and then paint a wave on it. Fill the box with sand.

5 Paint the skewer blue or white. Insert one end into the base of the whale.

6 Stand the whale in the box. You can make a zebra, too, following the same basic directions.

Animal Frames

With some cardboard, pipe cleaners, and a few beads you can make these funny picture holders.

1

Draw the giraffe with its frame as shown. Cut out the giraffe as well as a square in the middle.

2

Paint the giraffe. Let it dry. Cut a square from the cardboard the same size as the giraffe's body. Paint it black. When it's dry, glue it to the back of frame.

3

Insert pipe cleaners into the head and the bottom of the frame. Attach beads to the ends of the pipe cleaners and glue them in place.

MATERIALS

- Corrugated cardboard
- Acrylic paint and paintbrushes
- Scissors and art knife
- Pipe cleaners
- Glue
- Wood or plastic beads

Bubble Wrap Crocodile

This crocodile is easy to make out of a sheet of bubble wrap and some cardboard.

Roll the bubble wrap into a tube that is narrow at one end. This is your crocodile's body. Slip a 5-inch piece of wire into the narrow end, which is the tail. Tape the bubble wrap underneath the crocodile so it doesn't unroll. Bend the tail.

1

Paint the body with green acrylic paint, and then add a few touches of yellow. Let it dry.

2

3

Cut four feet out of corrugated cardboard and paint them green. Cut the crest out of red cardboard. Cut a slit in the back of the crocodile.

4

Apply glue to the red crest and insert into the slit. Glue the feet to the bottom of the crocodile. Glue on the eyes and paint the pupils black.

Funny Folded Animals

A giraffe, a tiger, an elephant…It's a Noah's ark of miniature animals! They're easy to put together and fun to play with. You can even build them a theater and put on shows for your friends!

MATERIALS

- White or colored construction paper
- Poster paint
- Paintbrushes
- Pencil
- Markers
- Glue
- Scissors

1 Draw the different pieces for the animal on white paper, including the eyes and mouth. Mark the slits as shown.

2 Cut out all the pieces, including the slits.

3

Paint your animal. Use a photo for inspiration, or just use your imagination!

Paint a shoebox to make a theater for your animals. You can make the other animals you see here, using the same techniques as shown for the giraffe.

4

Glue on the mouth and eyes. Use a black marker for the pupils.

5

Fold the giraffe's head.

6

Slide the tailpiece through the body of the giraffe as shown. Bend the headpiece and pass the neck through it.

Tube Fish

MATERIALS

- Empty cosmetic, cream, or shampoo tubes
- Scissors
- Foam sheets in assorted colors
- Acrylic paint
- Paintbrushes
- Black marker
- Self-hardening modeling clay
- Metal wire
- Glue
- Stapler

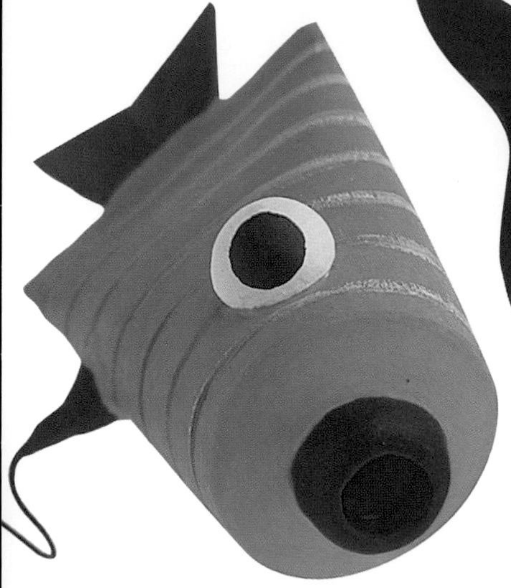

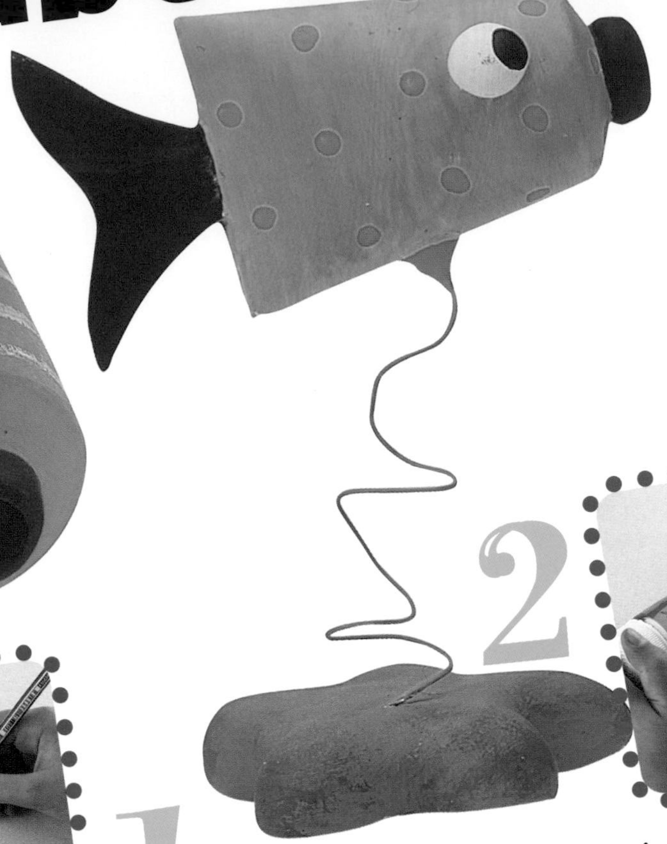

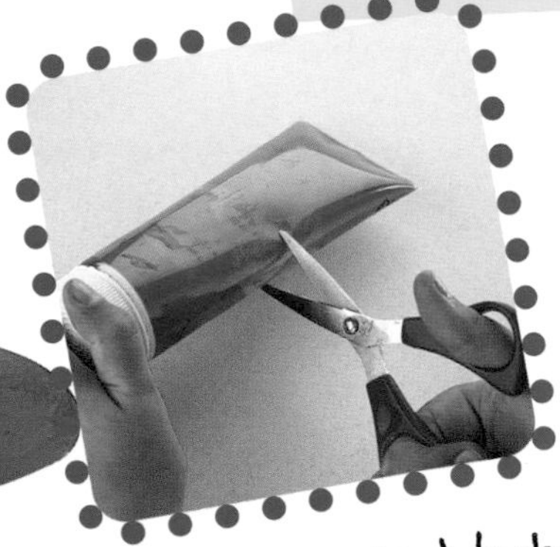

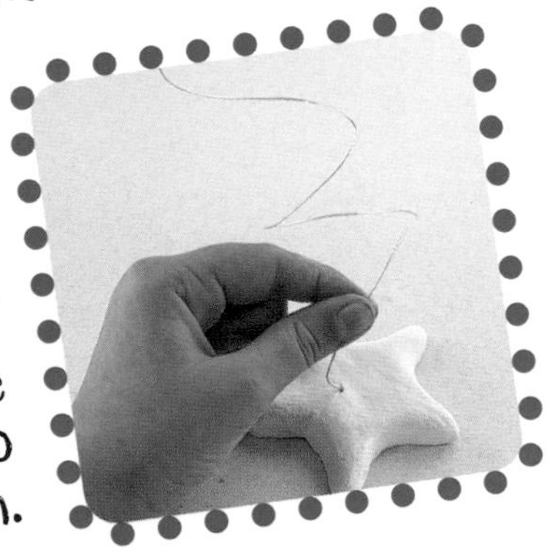

1

Draw a tail on a foam sheet and cut it out.

2

Cut the cosmetic tube in half. Wash it out and remove the cap. Staple the tail to the end of the tube.

3

Make a starfish out of modeling clay. Curl the wire and insert it into the fish and the starfish.

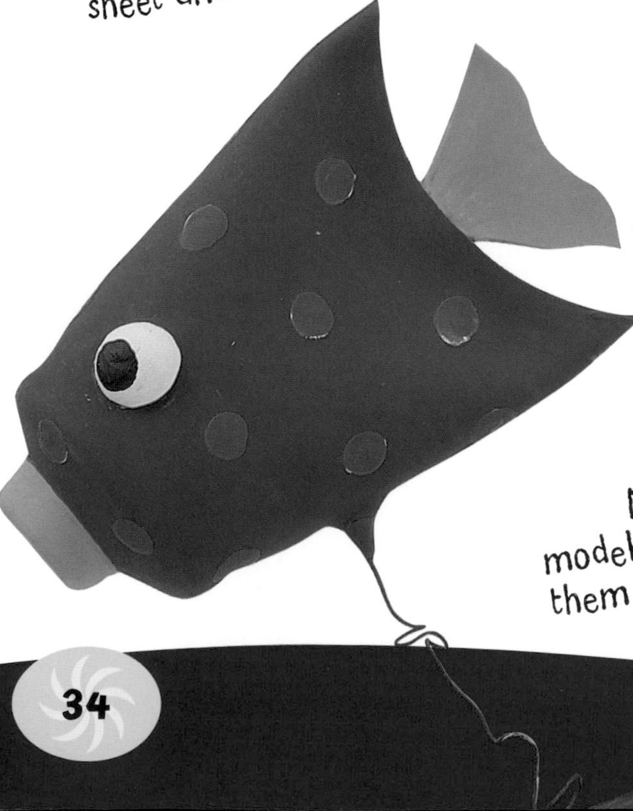

4

Make eyes out of modeling clay and glue them on. Paint the fish and the starfish.

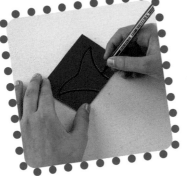

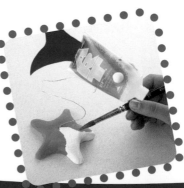

Paperweight Fish

These plaster fish look like the smooth stones you find in rivers or on beaches. They make nice paperweights to give as gifts.

MATERIALS

- Plaster of Paris
- Cooking oil
- Large spoon
- Empty plastic container
- Pencil
- Poster paint
- Paintbrushes

1 Follow the instructions for making the plaster. Mix it up in the plastic container.

2 Coat the spoon with a little oil. Fill the spoon with plaster and hold it level.

3 Let the plaster harden, remove it from the spoon and let it dry well.

4 Draw your fish design on the plaster.

5 Paint the background colors first. Let the paint dry. Use a fine paintbrush for the little details.

Your fish will look best if you use bright colors and vivid designs. Remember to protect the table with newspapers and wear an apron as you work.

35

Animal Magnets

Happy hens and playful pigs... Here are some fridge magnets you can make yourself. They're sure to brighten up the kitchen and bring a smile to everyone's face!

1

Form the body out of a small ball of modeling dough.

2

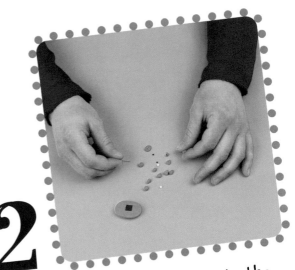

Press the magnet into the animal's back.

MATERIALS

- Oven-hardening modeling clay in assorted colors
- Toothpicks
- Bits of wire or paper clips
- Magnets

3

Form the rest of the pieces: feet, eyes, nose or beak, or wings.

4

Use a toothpick to help you handle the small pieces. If making the hen, bend wire and insert to make legs.

5

Assemble the animals and put them on a baking sheet. Ask a grown-up to help you bake them according to package instructions.

Snapping Animals

Crocodiles, toads and dinosaurs... These funny animals may look friendly, but watch out, they snap!

MATERIALS

- Green and white construction paper
- Sheet of white paper
- Pencil
- Black marker
- Poster paint and brushes
- Wooden clothespins
- Glue
- Scissors

Make sure your
clothespins are very
clean before you
paint them.
Be sure to use
wooden clothespins,
not plastic.

1

Copy the jaw's template, shown at right, onto green construction paper. Cut out the pieces.

2

Fold the green pieces to form the crocodile's jaws.

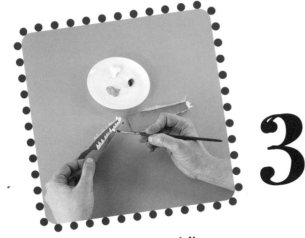

3

Paint the teeth white.

4

Paint the clothespin green and let dry. Glue the jaws to the closed ends of the clothespin.

5

Draw the eyes in black marker, cut them out and glue them on.

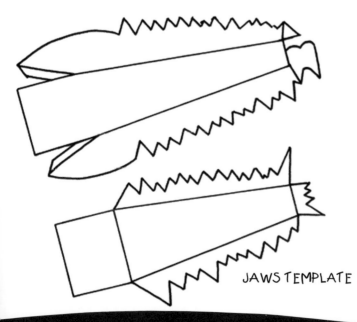

HINT

Make sure the paint is dry before you put the pieces together and glue them on. Add a drop of glue to the tip of the clothespin, wait a minute, then add another drop before you attach the jaw to it.

JAWS TEMPLATE

Animal Puppets

A lion, a bird, a monkey... These colorful wild animals are made out of cereal boxes and construction paper. You can use our models, or invent your own animals using the same technique.

MATERIALS

- Small cereal box
- Colored construction paper
- Black marker
- Glue
- Scissors and art knife
- Styrofoam ball
- Googly eyes
- Feathers

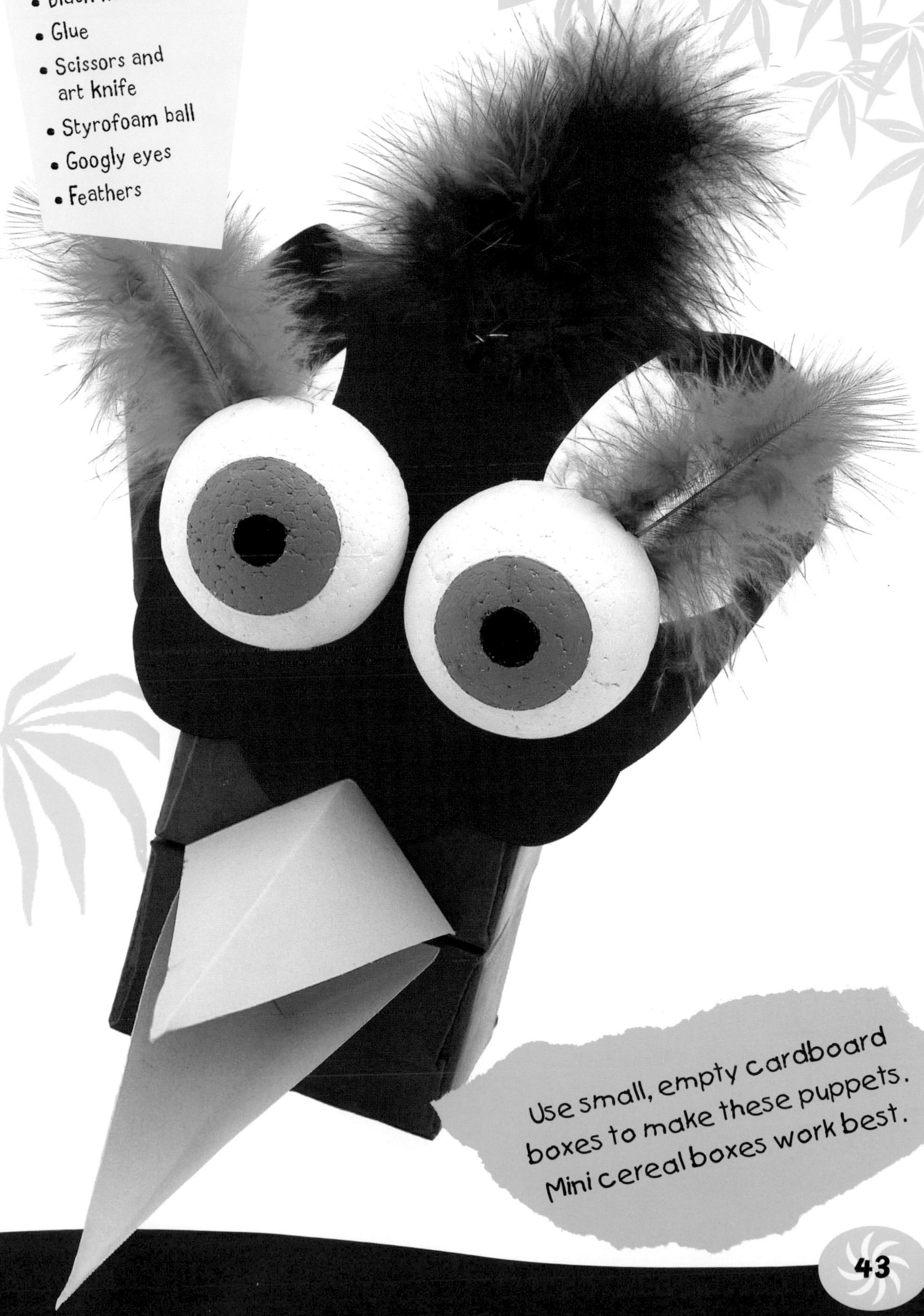

Use small, empty cardboard boxes to make these puppets. Mini cereal boxes work best.

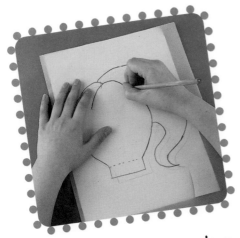

Using the black marker, draw the head on yellow construction paper and the lips on purple construction paper. Cut them out.

1

Make a tongue out of green construction paper. Cut the tip into a point and fold the tongue into accordion pleats.

2

3

Paint the box red.

SOURCES OF INSPIRATION

Find pictures of jungle animals in books or look at cartoon drawings and comic strips to give you ideas.

4 Use the art knife to cut the box down the middle on three sides. Don't cut through the back! Fold it in half. Cut the Styrofoam ball in two for the eyeballs and glue on googly eyes.

5

Glue on the lips and tongue, the feathers, and the eyeballs.

HAVE FUN NAMING YOUR PUPPETS
Give your animals names and make up a story about them. Then hide under a table and put on a puppet show!

Foam Animals

This funny zebra and silly giraffe are easy to make out of poster board paper and foam. Take them outside to play on the grass or decorate your room with them.

1

Fold a piece of poster board in half. Draw the zebra's body on one half. Draw the head and tail on a separate piece of poster board. Use the picture below as a guide.

2

Fold the poster board for the body in half as shown. Cut out the body. Cut out the head and tail.

MATERIALS

- Poster board
- Craft foam sheets
- Scissors
- Glue
- Fine-tip black marker

3 Cut the stripes, muzzle, hooves, and teeth out of foam.

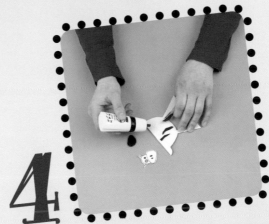

4 Glue the foam pieces onto the body, head and legs. Glue on the head and tail.

5 Unfold the board. Your animal will stand alone on its feet.

CAREFUL!
Not all glues work on foam. Choose a solvent-free glue that's made to use on plastic.

Accordion Critters

These animals make fun table decorations you can play with at your next party!

✂ **MATERIALS**

- Sheet of white paper
- Sheet of heavy white construction paper
- Paint and paintbrushes
- Scissors
- 2 wooden skewers
- All-purpose glue
- Pencil

1 Draw the head and the tail on two identical squares of construction paper. Paint and decorate them.

2 Cut out the head and tail as shown.

3 Cut out a long paper rectangle, and paint it the same color as the head and tail. Fold it into small accordion pleats.

4 Glue the head and tail to the accordion-folded paper. Hold them on with clothespins until the glue dries.

5 Glue one wooden skewer onto the back of the head and another one on the tail.

Spiral Snakes

These snakes make cool party decorations and take just minutes to make.

MATERIALS

- Construction paper in assorted colors
- Glue
- Scissors
- Black marker
- Thread and tape

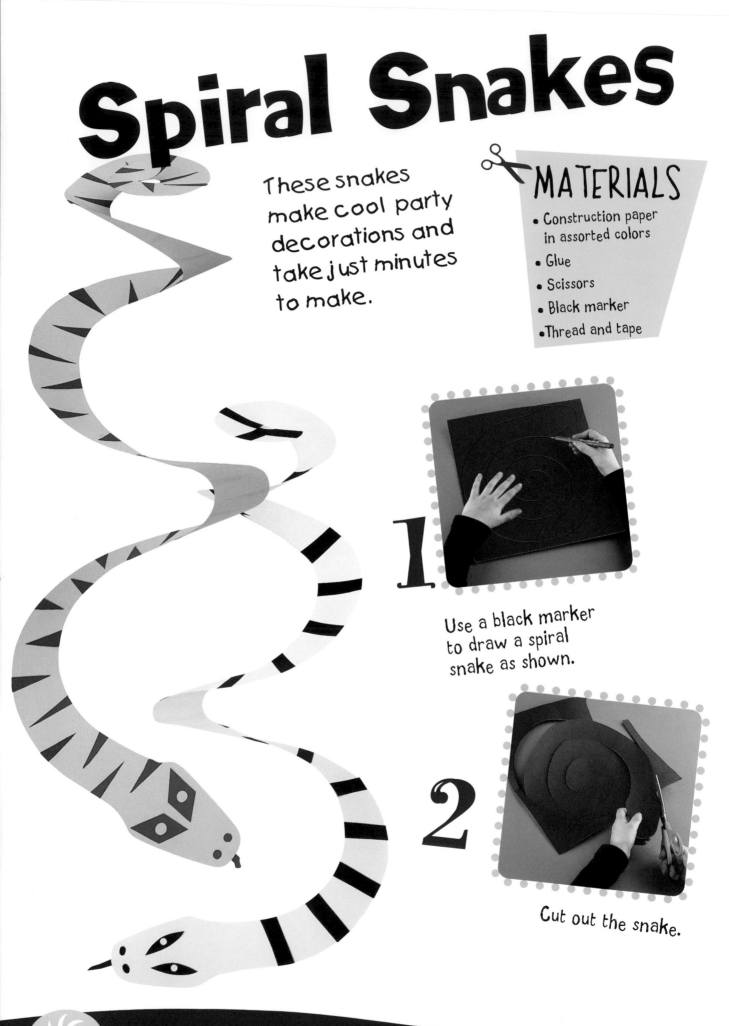

1 Use a black marker to draw a spiral snake as shown.

2 Cut out the snake.

3

On a different sheet of colored paper, draw small shapes like circles or triangles to decorate your snake. Using the model as a guide, draw eyes, a tongue and nostrils. Cut out all the pieces.

4

Glue all the pieces onto your snake. Attach a long thread to make a hanging string.

BE A SNAKE CHARMER!
Hang up your spiral snake
and watch it twist in the air!

Finger Puppets

A little newspaper, glue and paint, and you'll have a family of puppets to dance on your fingers! Make up a story for the donkey, the rabbit, the cat and the goose. Then put on a show!

MATERIALS

- Thick white paper
- Newspaper
- Adhesive tape
- White glue
- Pencil
- Scissors
- Paint
- Paintbrushes

1

As shown, draw rectangles that are long enough to wrap around a finger. Make sure you draw ears for the type of animal you want—draw long ears for a rabbit and shorter ones for a cat. Cut out the shapes.

2

Roll each shape around your index finger. Fasten with adhesive tape, but don't wrap them too tightly.

3

Tear little strips of newspaper and soak them in glue. Cover the puppets completely in layers of newspaper. Let dry.

4

Apply a thick coat of white paint. Let dry. Paint the puppets in bright colors. Add details with a fine paintbrush.

ARTISTIC CRAFTS

ARTISTIC CRAFTS

Ink Spot Animals

Calligraphy is an ancient Chinese and Japanese form of drawing and writing. Using China ink and a special pen with a metal tip, you can make delicate and precise designs. You can also transform your ink spots into fantastic animals.

MATERIALS

- Smooth white drawing paper
- Black China ink
- Paintbrushes
- Ink pen with fine and broad tips
- Cloth

1

Make ink spots of different sizes on your sheet of paper. Splatter the rest of your page with little drops of ink.

2

Using your pen nib, spread the ink and join some of the spots together to make the body of an animal in silhouette.

If you're making a bird, add feet, a tail, wings and a long beak. You can liven up your picture by transforming some of the other small dots into spiders, a sun, or plants, for example.

You can also draw animals on spotted paper, cut them out and frame them.

Splatter Painting

Spraying, splattering and splashing paint... this "drip technique" of painting was developed by American artist Jackson Pollock. It involves using a paintbrush to flick paint onto a canvas lying on the floor — without letting your brush touch the canvas!

1 Prepare your paint colors in bowls. Add enough water to make the paint thin and liquidy. Load a brush with paint.

2 Using Pollock's drip technique, spatter paint onto the paper by flicking the paintbrush at it.

3 You can also use a toothbrush. Dip it in paint and then spray the paper by running your finger across the bristles.

4

Make two drip paintings and let dry. On one, trace an edge half an inch wide around the border, then trace lines from top to bottom that are spaced 1 inch apart.

5

Cut strips to the lines, being careful not to cut the border.

6

On the other painting, trace and cut out strips that are 1 inch apart.

7

Take these strips and weave them in and out of the strips on the first painting.

8

Finish off your new work of art by pasting it onto black cardboard.

Paul Jackson Pollock was born in 1912 and died in 1956. During one of his trips across the country, Pollock discovered the "sand painting" technique of the Native Americans. He also was inspired by artists like Picasso, Miró, and Masson.

Mosaic Cards

Make your own colorful and original mosaic art to put on greeting cards.

①

Fold a sheet of colored construction paper in half to make a card. Draw your design on the front.

✂ ## MATERIALS

- Shells from 2 hard-boiled eggs
- Colored construction paper
- Paint
- Fine paintbrush
- Scissors
- Glue

②

Apply glue inside the design.

3

Lay the eggshells on top of the glue.

4

Press the eggshells down to stick them to the paper. Use the cap of a tube of paint to press the shells flat. Let dry.

5

Paint the shells with thin, watered-down paint in different colors. Finish decorating your card by gluing strips of colored construction paper near the borders.

Optical Illusions

You can create amazing optical effects with just a sheet of paper and a marker. All you need to draw these geometric figures is a little patience.

Notice how you have a sense of a 3-D pyramid in the final drawing? Depending on how you look at it, the small square either seems to be down in the bottom of a hollow pyramid, or sitting at the top.

1 Draw a square. Mark each side: A on the left, B on the bottom, C on the top and D on the right.

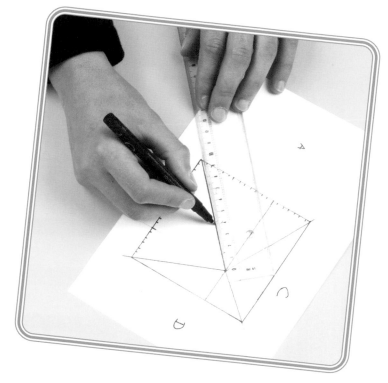

2 Draw a diagonal line across from corner AB to corner CD. Draw a diagonal line from corner BD toward the middle of side C, stopping where it meets the first diagonal line. Draw a diagonal line from corner AC to where it meets the other two lines.

3 Paint or color black stripes as shown. The stripes in sections A and B should be half an inch wide, and the stripes in sections C and D should be a quarter of an inch wide. Paint or color a small black square where all four lines intersect.

Look at the middle of the drawing on the right. Rotate the sheet slowly. As it turns, colors seem to appear before your eyes!

Reflection Paintings

A river, a lake, the seashore...Choose a water landscape for your subject. Go outdoors or use a photo. Have fun drawing all the details that you see reflected in the water.

MATERIALS

- White drawing paper
- Colored pencils or pastels
- Poster paint
- Paintbrushes
- Pencil

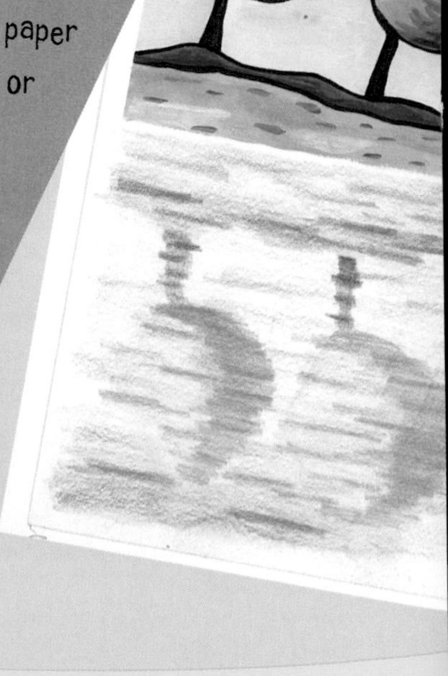

Trace a horizontal line across the sheet of paper to divide it in half.

Draw your landscape on the top half of the sheet.

Water down the poster paint and color in your landscape.

Use a pencil to draw the "reflection" of the landscape on the bottom half of the sheet. Create contrast between the two parts by shading in the reflection with colored pencils or pastels. Your shading strokes should be horizontal (from side to side).

Miniature Paintings

This is an easy way to try your hand at painting. Focus on a landscape, a still life, such as a bowl of fruit, or just imagine a scene. Work with bright, simple colors. Or create abstract shapes of what you see. Then finish your work with a frame in matching tones a true little masterpiece!

HELPFUL HINT
Don't try to do all the little details. Keep your shapes simple. Your picture should be more abstract than realistic. This is how most artists begin painting.

1

Start by drawing a box. Don't make it too large, because you want to keep your artwork small.

2

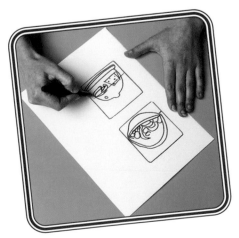

Draw your subject. Choose a bowl of fruit, a plate of cheese, or any object you like.

MATERIALS

- Drawing paper
- Markers
- Colored pencils
- Poster paint
- Paintbrushes
- Glue
- Scissors
- Ruler

3

Paint your picture. Choose a range of colors that are bright and that go well together.

4

On another piece of paper, paint a solid area that will become your frame.

5

Paint details on your frame. You can make tiny geometric designs or splatter paint with your paintbrush to make spots.

6

Cut your finished picture out, leaving a white border around the edge. Glue it to your frame.

Grid Drawings

With this grid technique that is often used for drawing, you can easily and accurately copy your favorite pictures in different sizes.

MATERIALS

- Drawing paper
- Tracing paper
- Pencil
- Eraser
- Ruler
- Paint
- Paintbrush
- Pastels, colored pencils or markers

The project will be easier if you photocopy the picture you want to reproduce, or lay a sheet of tracing paper over it.

1

Lay a sheet of tracing paper over your picture. Use a ruler and pencil to draw a grid on it, with each square measuring half an inch. Number each square from left to right and from top to bottom.

2

Draw the same grid on a piece of drawing paper. Keep the same number of squares. You can change the size of the squares, depending on how big you'd like your drawing to be. If you want your drawing to be twice the size of the original picture, for example, make your squares 1 inch in size instead of half an inch.

3

Reproduce the picture on the drawing paper. Copy what you see in each square of the original picture into its corresponding square on your drawing paper.

4

Once your drawing is finished, erase the grid, being careful not to erase your drawing.

5

Add color to your drawing. You can use poster or acrylic paint, pastels, colored pencils or markers.

Torn Paper Portraits

Whether you make a caricature or a portrait, you'll enjoy working with torn paper. Many artists have used this technique, so why not try your hand at it?

MATERIALS

- Various kinds of paper
- White drawing paper
- Large sheet of colored cardboard
- Pencil, wax or wood crayons, markers
- Poster paint and paintbrushes
- Glue

You'll notice that this technique of tearing paper gives your portrait a special texture and a sense of volume. Above all, try to give your character its own personality, rather than trying to copy the model you see here.

Your portrait will be more artistic if you mix different textures of paper together — smooth with rough, thick with thin, transparent with opaque. You can even add extra color or texture to your paper by painting it or coloring it in crayon before you tear it up.

1

Paint or color several pieces of paper, using a different technique on each one. For example, you can use a wide paintbrush that leaves lines on the paper, shade another piece of paper in wax or pencil crayon and color another in marker.

2

Tear shapes out of the different sheets of paper to make up your portrait.

3

Paint a sheet of drawing paper in a skin color, let it dry, then tear out the shape of a head. Draw a face on it in pencil. Glue the head to a sheet of cardboard torn at the edges. Arrange the torn paper shapes to make your portrait.

4

When you are satisfied with the way your character looks, carefully glue the pieces of paper onto the face and cardboard. Glue the cardboard to another sheet of colored cardboard to frame it.

Paper Cut-out Paintings

✂ MATERIALS

- Large pieces of paper
- Poster paint and paint roller
- Pencil
- Scissors
- Glue

Abstract Plant Design

1 Use a paint roller to roll out the different colors of paint you have chosen. Let the paint dry well.

2 Find inspiration in nature, like leaves and seaweed, for example, to create your designs.

3 Draw the shapes you want on the painted paper. Cut them out. Glue your shapes onto poster board in an interesting pattern.

The French artist Henri Matisse was a master at turning simple cut-outs into amazing abstract art. His collages consisted of pieces of paper painted in strong, warm colors, cut into stylized shapes, and assembled into interesting patterns and scenes. Why not try your hand at Matisse-style collage? Here are two examples for you to imitate.

Abstract Shapes

1 Cut irregular geometric shapes out of brightly colored paper.

2 Compose an abstract picture using pieces of paper. Glue them onto a sheet of white paper and then onto colored cardboard as shown.

Chinese Painting

Discover the ancient technique of Chinese ink painting. Draw simple lines that you see in nature, as if you were writing in calligraphy. See how the ink and water flow into new shapes and shadings.

MATERIALS

- A special paintbrush for calligraphy
- A bowl of water
- Chinese ink
- A scrap of thick paper to test shadings
- Watercolor paper

1

Dilute a little Chinese ink in some water to make a light gray. Check its lightness by brushing it on a sheet of thick paper.

2

Use this light gray color to paint a branch, along with its smaller branches, on your watercolor paper.

Be careful! If you want to darken an area that has already been painted, wait for the paper to dry first to prevent smudging, then go over it again.

Add more ink to the water to darken it. Outline the branch and add some shading, using downward strokes.

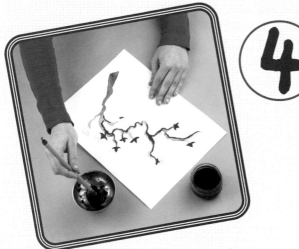

Use black ink that is not diluted to add shadows and to make the base of the blooms.

Paint the rest of the blooms in watered-down ink.

Once you have mastered the technique, try painting a landscape. Be careful where you place your ink to create lighter and darker areas.

DID YOU KNOW?
The Chinese and Japanese art of writing with ink is known as calligraphy. Calligraphy means "beautiful writing."

Impressionist Painting

MATERIALS

- Kraft paper
- Poster paint in assorted colors
- Paintbrushes
- Rags

If you ever look at the paintings of artist Claude Monet up close, you'll see that they're made of tiny splotches of paint. These splotches of many different colors don't blend together until you look at the painting from farther away. Monet's brush strokes and the way he combined light and dark colors helped to create shadows, light and reflections in his paintings.

1 Unroll the kraft paper on your work surface and hold it in place with repositionable tape. You may find that it is easier to do this on the floor.

2

Start by painting some light blue and dark blue splotches, which will be the light in your painting. Add a splotch of yellow for the sun.

3

For the water lilies, paint spots of lighter and darker green. Shade the background blue in the same way. Add some light spots to the background, using white paint with a tiny bit of yellow and green mixed into it.

4

Your painting is ready to be put on display – you just need to give it a title. It can be inspired by a place or a time of day – the way Claude Monet used to name his paintings!

Tie-dye Paper

Tie-dye designs are usually seen on t-shirts, but you can have fun with this technique to make your own original gift-wrap!

Yellow Design

MATERIALS

- White and light-colored tissue paper
- Ink in assorted colors
- Scissors
- Paper towels

1

Fold a sheet of tissue paper into a strip, and then fold it into accordion pleats that are about 2 to 3 inches wide.

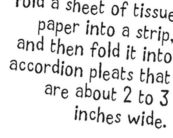

2

Prepare two bowls of ink, one red and one green. Quickly dip one corner of the folded-up tissue paper in green ink. Blot the excess ink with paper towels.

Dip the opposite corner in green ink, and the other two corners in red ink. Blot them the same way.

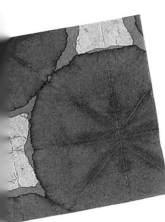

Carefully unfold the tissue paper and let it dry. You can press it between two sheets of ordinary paper if it is crumpled.

White Design

Fold a square sheet of tissue paper so the four corners meet in the middle. Fold the sheet in half, and then in half again, to make a square.

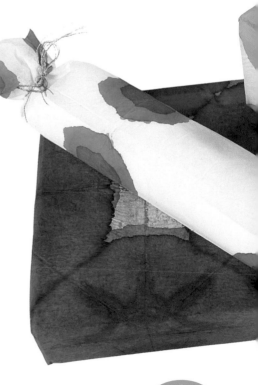

Dip each of the four corners in a bowl of ink. Blot them on paper towel.

Unfold the tissue paper, let it dry, and then smooth it out.

PAPER CRAFTS

PAPER CRAFTS

Elegant Cards

MATERIALS

- Construction paper in assorted colors
- Colored translucent paper
- Scissors
- Glue
- Gold and silver paint pens
- Gold ribbon, cord or string

These sparkling cards look expensive and are easy to make. All you need is colored construction paper, translucent paper and a paint pen.

Translucent Cards

1

Fold a sheet of translucent paper in half to make a card that measures 4 inches by 6 inches.

2

Cut two 1-inch by 5-inch rectangles out of construction paper in two different colors.

 3 Glue the two pieces of construction paper side by side inside the card.

4 Decorate the cover of the card with gold paint designs. Let dry.

Sparkling Cards

1 Cut and fold cards out of colored construction paper. Draw gold or silver paint designs on them. Let dry.

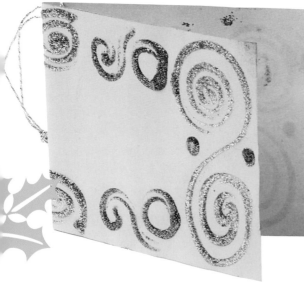

2 Cut a piece of gold of ribbon, string or cord that is more than double the length of the fold. Tie the cord around the fold of the card.

Halloween Pop-up Cards

Invite your friends to your Halloween party with this pop-up card. A monster or ghost will pop out when they open it!

MATERIALS

- Colored construction paper in black, white, red, purple, green, and yellow
- Envelopes
- Pencil
- Scissors
- Glue
- Regular and double-sided tape
- Small metal springs

1 Fold a sheet of black construction paper in two. Cut it so it will fit into the envelope. Draw your character on white or colored construction paper.

HINT
Use this → space for your party information or greeting.

2

Draw and cut the other features (eyes, nose, teeth, etc.) out of different colored construction paper.

4

Glue the features onto your character.

3

You can use our models for inspiration. Use tracing paper if you want to copy them.

5

Stick the spring to the double-sided tape and attach the back of your character to the spring with regular tape.

6

Close the card, press down firmly on it and put it in the envelope. When you open the card the monster will pop out!

Bewitching Cards

The moon is up and the witches and bats are ready to fly! Here are some eye-catching cards to make for Halloween.

1

Cut a 6 inches square out of colored construction paper.

✂ MATERIALS

- Orange, violet and black construction paper
- Black and orange raffia
- Large embroidery needle
- Hole punch
- Scissors
- Art knife
- Ruler
- Pencil
- Glue

2

Draw your design (a witch, bat, moon or star) and cut it out with an art knife.

3

Cut a 5 inches square out of black construction paper. Measure and cut strips that are half an inch wide, being careful to stop half an inch before the edge of the construction paper.

4

Measure and cut strips of construction paper that are 6 inches long by half an inch wide in a different color. Cut them out.

6

Lay the construction paper with your cutout design on top of the black construction paper. Use a hole punch to make a hole every half inch around the edge. Thread a strand of raffia through the holes and tie it into a bow at the end.

5

Weave these strips in and out of the black construction paper as shown.

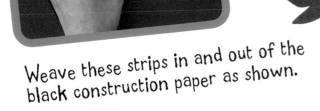

Paper Cut-out Gift Tags

Use this paper cut-out technique to make decorative invitations or gift cards.

1

Cut a 6 inch by 8 inch rectangle out of pink cardboard. Fold in half to make a 4 inch by 6 inch card.

2

Cut a 3 inch by 5 inch rectangle out of blue cardboard. Fold in half so that it measures 1 ½ inches by 5 inches. Cut out spirals or triangles along the folded edge.

3

Unfold the blue cardboard and glue it to the center of the pink cardboard as shown.

4

If it will be a gift card, use a hole punch to make a hole in one of the corners, at the fold. Loop a piece of gold string or ribbon through the hole and tie it to your gift.

Heart Notebook

You can keep precious souvenirs, notes, and photos in this heart-shaped notebook.

✂ MATERIALS

- 20 sheets of yellow paper
- 2 sheets of cardboard
- Yellow, red and white construction paper
- 2 metal key rings or paper fasteners
- Hole punch
- Glue
- Ribbon
- Pencil
- Small padlock

1

Put two pieces of cardboard together and cut out a large heart.

2

Fold 20 sheets of yellow paper in half to use as notebook filling. Make sure the paper will fit inside the heart covers. If not, trim the edges.

3

Punch two holes in the paper. Then punch two holes in the hearts that will line up with the paper.

4

With the paper between the hearts and all the holes matching up, attach the notebook together with two key rings or paper fasteners.

5

Decorate the cover with more hearts and ribbons.

HINT
Make your creation a secret diary by punching a hole and adding a padlock.

You can make a rectangular notebook, too!

Japanese Kimono Cards

Fold origami paper into a series of beautiful Japanese kimono cards.

MATERIALS

- Origami paper
- Construction paper
- Pencil
- Black and red markers
- Glue
- Scissors
- Ruler

DID YOU KNOW ?

The Japanese traditional clothing called a kimono is made of only one piece of fabric.

1

Fold a sheet of origami paper along the vertical lines, and then along the diagonal lines as shown at right.

2

Draw the face, hands and feet on colored construction paper and cut them out. Draw the wig on black paper and cut it out.

3

4

Draw the eyes and nose with a black marker. Use a red marker to draw the mouth.

Glue all the pieces onto a sheet of colored cardboard folded in two to make a card.

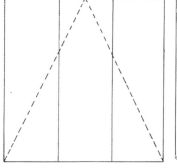

On the back of the square sheet of origami paper, use a ruler to trace two vertical lines that will divide the sheet into three equal sections. Trace a triangle from the top center point of the paper down to the bottom corners.

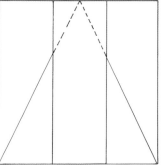

Cut along the two diagonal lines that are colored blue in the diagram. Do not cut the part where the lines are dotted.

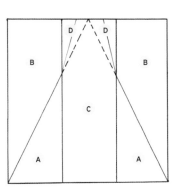

Write letters on each section as shown. Fold A over C toward the center. Fold B over D toward the outside. Fold B diagonally toward the back (following the blue lines on the diagram).

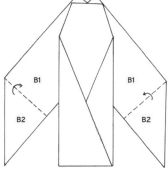

Fold B2 over B1 along the dotted lines.

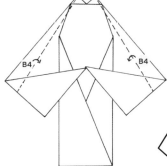

Fold B4 toward the inside along the dotted lines.

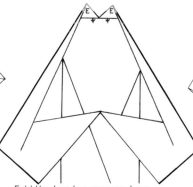

Fold the two top corners down.

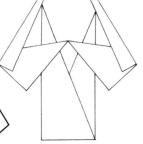

Turn the kimono over. This is the front of the kimono.

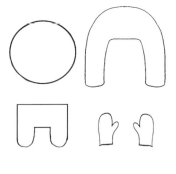

Quick and Colorful Cards

With simple shapes cut out of cardboard and some yarn or string, you can make these colorful and original cards.

1 Cut a sheet of colored cardboard in half. Fold it in half to make the card.

2 Draw balloons on three different colors of cardboard.

MATERIALS

- Paper in an assortment of bright colors
- Colored yarn or string
- Glue
- Scissors
- Pencil

3 Cut out the balloons.

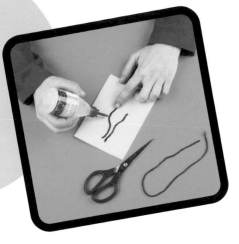

4 Glue three pieces of yarn or string to the front of the card.

5 Glue the balloons to the tops of the strings. You can make other cards using our models for inspiration.

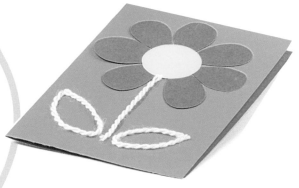

GAME CRAFTS

GAMES

Dancing Monsters

Striped, polka-dotted or downright creepy, here are some mischievous monster puppets to make out of paper. Let your imagination run wild when you design your characters. You'll need a little patience when it's time to fold their legs!

Choose bright, contrasting paper colors to make your monsters really stand out. And remember, the scarier the better!

MATERIALS

- Glossy colored construction paper
- Glue
- Scissors
- Nylon thread
- Markers
- Paint
- Paintbrushes

1 Draw the shape of your monster with a marker. If you want to make a big monster, its head should take up an entire sheet of paper. Cut out the shape just outside the lines.

2

3 Cut strips of paper that are 1 inch wide and the length of your sheet.

Use your imagination when you paint your monster. Bright, contrasting colors look best.

Glue the ends of two strips together in an "L", and then fold one across the other, over and over, for the entire length.

4

5 Make the other leg the same way, and then glue them to the back of the monster's head. Punch a small hole at the top of the head and tie a long piece of nylon thread to it.

BECOME A MONSTER TAMER
Practice your performance before the show—and don't reveal how you made your puppets! If you hold the nylon threads inside your sleeves, it will be easier to hold them up and make them dance!

Make the monster's legs super-long by making an extra set of legs and then attaching them to the first set. Just remember, the smaller the puppet, the harder it will be to make!

NAMING THEM IS FUN, TOO!

Wart-face, Fang, Eye-Popper... Once you've made your monster, have fun thinking of a silly name. Think gross! Think weird!

Fishing Game

Have your party guests "catch" their own favors with this fun game.

MATERIALS

- Corrugated cardboard
- Art knife or scissors
- Pencil
- Black marker
- Acrylic paints
- Paintbrush
- Paper clips
- Yarn

1

Draw fish in different shapes on a sheet of paper.

2

Trace the best ones on corrugated cardboard, using a black marker.

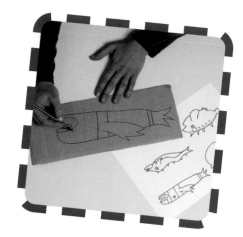

3

Paint the fish in bright colors. Let them dry and then cut them out.

4

Bend a paper clip to make a hook. Tie it to a long strand of yarn that is attached to a stick. Pierce a hole in each fish's back and insert another paper clip.

5

Prepare batches of prizes, like different candies or small toys. Assign each type of prize its own number. Then paint a number on the back of the fish. When someone "catches" a fish, award them their corresponding prize. Happy fishing!

HINT
To make the game more challenging, give each player a small pail or bucket. The first one to fill their bucket with goodies wins a big prize. The pails make great goodie bags!

The Wiggling Nose

Pointy or twisted, wiggling or stretching... transform your character's nose with a wave of your hand!

MATERIALS

- White cardboard
- Colored construction paper
- Pencil
- Black marker
- Scissors
- Black beads
- Black thread
- Glue
- Poster paint

1 Draw your character's profile, skipping the nose, on white cardboard.

Shake your picture gently to make hundreds of funny faces!

2 String a bunch of black beads on a 4- to 5-inch long thread.

3 Punch a hole at the top and at the bottom of your profile. Pass the ends of the thread through the holes and tape them at the back.

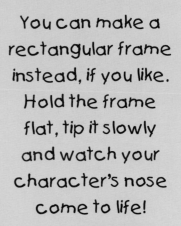

You can make a rectangular frame instead, if you like. Hold the frame flat, tip it slowly and watch your character's nose come to life!

The Frame

2

Lay it on your drawing, trace the outline, and then cut off the excess paper. Paint your frame and decorate it with paper cut-outs or stickers.

1

Cut an oval frame out of white cardboard.

3

Glue the frame to your drawing. Glue another sheet of cardboard to the back of your drawing to hide the threads.

Cartoon Book

Funny faces, bizarre bodies, and laughable legs... These cartoon characters change before your eyes — all you have to do is turn the pages!

✂ MATERIALS

- Sheets of white paper
- Marker
- Ruler
- Scissors

1 Stack three sheets of paper on top of one another. Fold them into three equal sections across the widest part of the paper.

2 Use the ruler to divide the sheets into three equal sections across the narrower part of the paper. Mark off the sections in pencil.

3 Draw a funny cartoon character in the middle section. The head should be in the top part, the body in the middle and the legs in the bottom section.

Cut through all the paper along your pencil lines. Do not cut the middle section.

Fold over one section at a time and draw a head, body, and legs for other characters, until all the pages are full.

Your book is done. All you have to do is turn the pages in different combinations to discover new cartoon characters.

115

People Cube Puzzles

It's a three-piece puzzle, but the pieces are six-sided cubes! Put them together in different combinations and you'll come up with some pretty funny characters!

HINT
Consider using heads from your favorite photos. See how silly your friends and family can look!

1

Get a block of Styrofoam. You can usually find one in a box that held an appliance or a computer. Cut three cubes of equal size out of it.

2

Use a cube to trace 18 squares out of 6 different colors of paper.

3

Glue the paper to the cubes, covering each side of the cube with a different color.

4

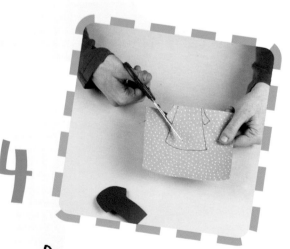

Draw six heads, six bodies with arms and six pairs of legs for different characters. Cut out all the parts of your characters.

5 Glue a face to each side of the first cube. Glue all the bodies onto the second cube and all the legs onto the third cube.

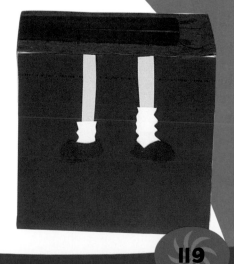

6 Add details with your colored markers, such as a handbag, stripes, flowers or numbers on a shirt.

7 Now make up different characters by stacking the cubes in different ways!

Feed the Frog

Challenge your friends to this skill-testing game. Hold the cup and then swing the bead so it falls inside — it's not as easy as it looks!

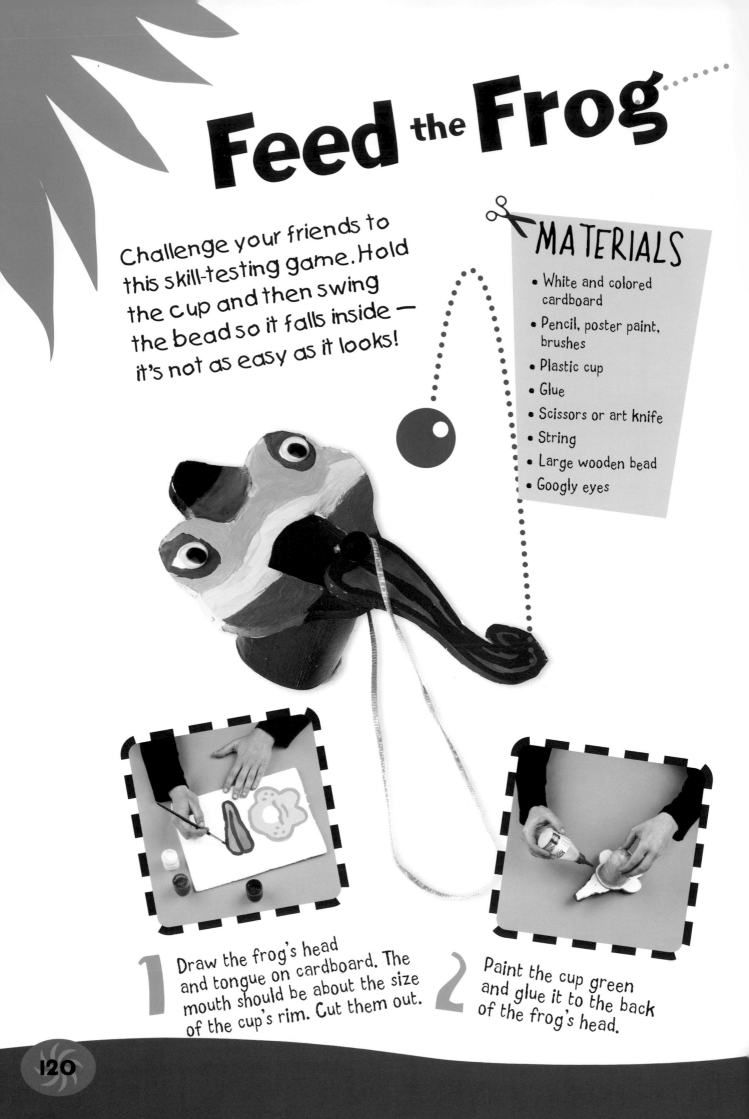

MATERIALS

- White and colored cardboard
- Pencil, poster paint, brushes
- Plastic cup
- Glue
- Scissors or art knife
- String
- Large wooden bead
- Googly eyes

1 Draw the frog's head and tongue on cardboard. The mouth should be about the size of the cup's rim. Cut them out.

2 Paint the cup green and glue it to the back of the frog's head.

3 Glue on the tongue and eyes. Tie one end of the string around the rim of the cup.

4 Attach the bead to the other end of the string and knot it in place.

Balloon Monsters

You can have a game of catch with these creatures and see how their faces change.

MATERIALS

- Flour
- Balloons
- Colored felt
- Scissors
- Funnel
- Googly eyes
- Glue

1 Use the funnel to fill the balloon with flour.

2 Tie the end of the balloon tightly.

3 Cut a smile, teeth or hair out of colored felt.

4

Glue them on, along with the googly eyes.

5

Make heads into funny shapes!

Draw Your Own Maze

Have fun drawing a picture that has a maze built into it. A maze is a path with one entrance, one exit, a few crossroads... and many dead ends! Can you get lost in it? Of course, but you're the designer of this ingenious and mysterious game!

MATERIALS

- A sheet of white paper
- Black markers

1

Draw the general outline of the maze picture in pencil. You can use this clown's head as an example, if you like.

2

Retrace the lines in black marker. Be careful not to cross the lines and to leave open paths in different areas of the drawing, for example, in the nose, mouth and eyes.

3 In each area, draw little mazes with an entrance and exit.

4 Fill in the empty spaces with more paths and draw the main entrance. In this example, it's under the chin.

5 Try tracing a path through your maze with a pencil and make sure you can get out! Imagine the mazes you can design inside other pictures.

DID YOU KNOW?

The earliest maze was described in an ancient Greek myth. The maze was home to the dreaded minotaur, a monster that was half-man, half-bull. Theseus defeated the minotaur and found his way out of the maze. The Romans often decorated the floors of their villas with maze designs of mosaic tile. Some city parks feature giant mazes made from hedges.

Silly Face People

A sly glance, a smile, a scowl, or funny face... You can change the expressions on your characters in the blink of an eye by sliding the strips of paper behind them.

MATERIALS

- Drawing paper
- Pencil
- Black and colored markers
- Ruler
- Glue
- Scissors
- Art knife

1

Fold a sheet of drawing paper in two like a book. Draw your character's head on the "front cover." Trace a rectangle where the eyes should be and another rectangle at the mouth.

2

Unfold the sheet. Make two cuts along the fold, at the same height as the eye and mouth sections. Cut out the two rectangles.

3

Cut two long strips of paper the same width as the rectangles you've cut out. On one strip draw different sets of eyes, and on the other draw different kinds of mouths.

4

Slide the strips of paper through the cuts in the fold. Fold the sheet closed and hold it in place with a few drops of glue. Now slide the eyes and mouth and see all the silly faces you can make.

Dragon Fortune-teller

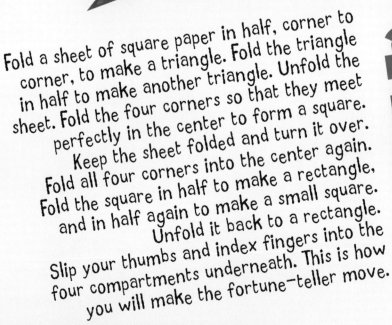

Dragons are a symbol of wisdom. See what this fun game has in store for you.

MATERIALS

- 2 sheets of paper
- Pencil
- Markers
- Scissors

1

Fold a sheet of square paper in half, corner to corner, to make a triangle. Fold the triangle in half to make another triangle. Unfold the sheet. Fold the four corners so that they meet perfectly in the center to form a square. Keep the sheet folded and turn it over. Fold all four corners into the center again. Fold the square in half to make a rectangle, and in half again to make a small square. Unfold it back to a rectangle. Slip your thumbs and index fingers into the four compartments underneath. This is how you will make the fortune-teller move.

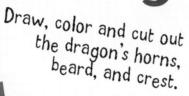

2

Use our model to help you draw the dragon face on the outside of the fortune-teller. Color it in with markers.

3

Draw, color and cut out the dragon's horns, beard, and crest.

4

Glue the pieces onto the dragon as shown in the photo.

5

Write a message in each of the compartments. Ask your friend to name a number. Move the fortune-teller with your fingers to count to that number. Have your friend pick a flap. Open the compartment to read the message inside.

Optical Illusions
Spinning Disks

Here are some optical illusions that are sure to make your head spin! Observe the differences between the two spirals and the sensation you get from each one as you watch it in motion...

On this drawing, there are two spirals, one inside the other. When you spin the disk, they seem to move in two directions at once.

On this drawing, there is only one kind of spiral. When you spin the disk, the spiral seems to move outward.

MATERIALS

- Photocopier
- Paper
- White cardboard
- Glue
- Scissors
- Paper clips

1 Use a photocopier to copy the two spirals shown here (or you can trace them). Cut out the photocopied spirals.

2 Cut two circles out of cardboard.

3 Glue your spiral onto the cardboard.

4 Straighten out a paper clip and stick one end into the back of the spiral disk at its center point.

5 Hold the paper clip between your hands. Rub your hands together to make the spiral spin and see what happens!

Greedy Monsters

These grimacing, hairy creatures have a strange smile... and they'll gobble up whatever you throw at them! Which one is greedier?

MATERIALS

- Shoeboxes
- Poster paint
- Black marker
- Sheet of white paper
- Styrofoam balls in assorted sizes
- Colored raffia
- Art knife
- Foam rubber ball
- All-purpose glue

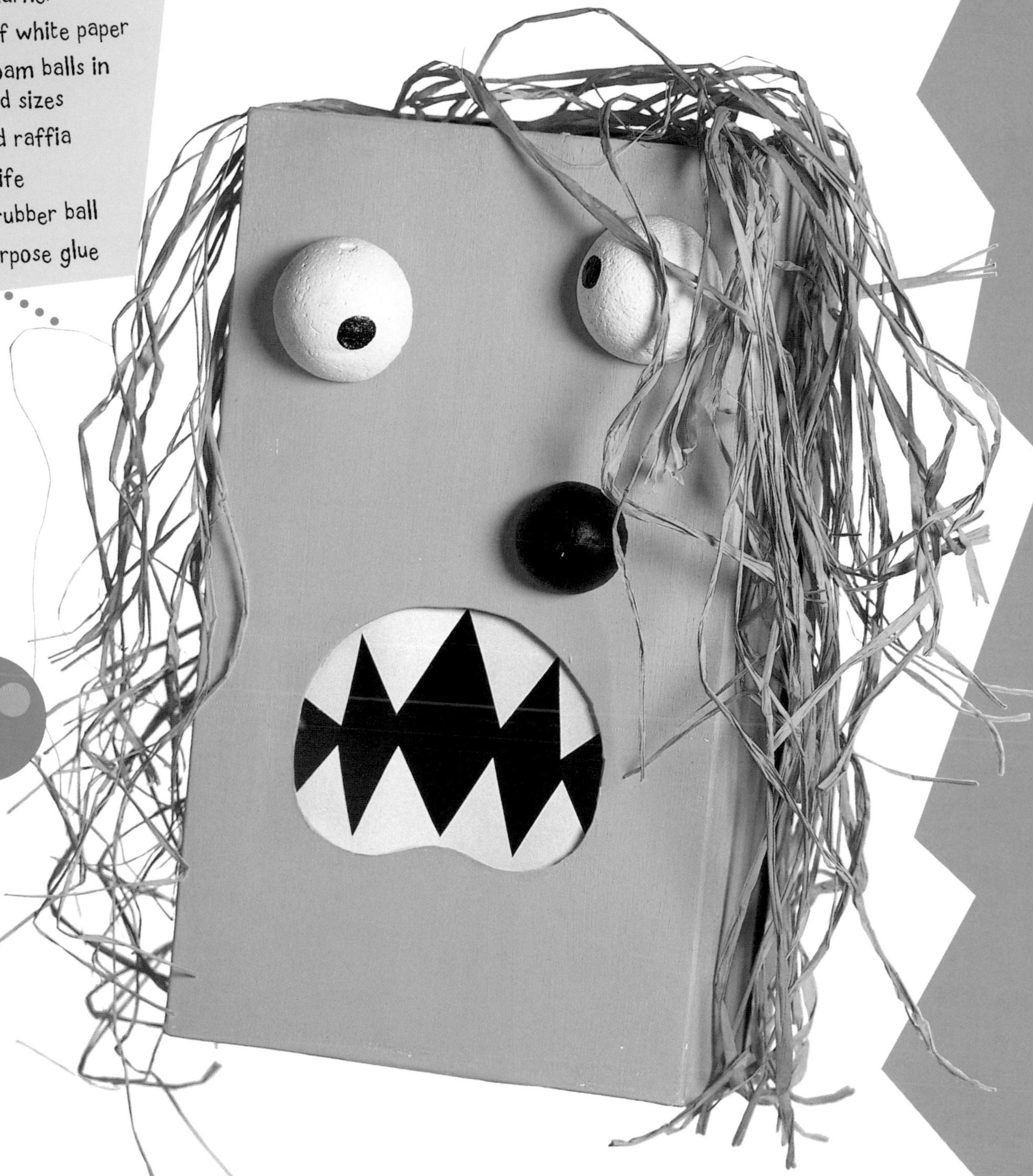

To play this game, don't use a ball that's too big. Use a small foam rubber or ping pong ball, and don't throw too hard! The object of the game is not to destroy the box, but to aim for the mouth!

The larger the mouth on the box, the easier the game will be to play. Making your box and decorating it, however, will take longer!

1

Use a marker to draw a mouth on the box.

2

Give the shoebox an undercoat of white paint.

3

Have an adult help you use scissors or an art knife to cut out the mouth.

4

Following our model, trace the teeth on a sheet of white paper and cut them out.

5

Ask an adult to cut the Styrofoam balls in half with an art knife.

6

Paint the box a color. Paint the nose and the pupils on the eyes black.

7

Glue raffia inside the lid to make hair.

8

Glue the eyes and nose to the box. Turn the box lid over and glue the teeth to the inside of the mouth.

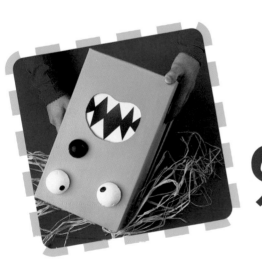

9

Close the box, stand it up against a wall, and start playing!

Each player has three tries. Whoever gets the ball into the mouth the most often wins.

GIFT CRAFTS

GIFT CRAFTS

Centipede Desk Organizer

No more pencils, pens, pins and papers cluttering up your desk! This cardboard centipede will help you keep it all in order.

1

Use the sponge to paint the insides of the rolls yellow, and the outsides green.

MATERIALS

- 12 empty toilet paper rolls
- Self-hardening modeling clay
- Small Styrofoam ball
- Acrylic paints
- Sponge
- Brushes
- Glue
- 2 small pieces of wire or pipe cleaners
- Marker
- Googly eyes

2

Paint the Styrofoam ball green.

3

Glue the rolls together so they form a zigzag. Glue the Styrofoam ball to the first roll to make the head.

4

Form 24 small balls of clay to make the feet. Let the clay dry, and then paint the feet yellow.

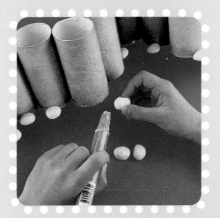

5

When the paint is dry, glue the feet to the bottoms of the rolls.

6

Cut two pieces of pipe cleaner for the antennae. Insert them into the head. Put two clay balls on the tips of the wire and paint them yellow. Draw a smile on the centipede with the marker. Glue on two googly eyes.

Magic Mirrors

Draw and paint an animal, a character or a landscape on the frame of a mirror. When you look into it, your reflection will be that of a princess, the middle of a flower, a cat's face, or maybe a space traveler! It's magic!

MATERIALS

- Mirror with a wide wooden frame
- Pencil
- Black marker
- Paint
- Paintbrushes
- Glitter glue pen
- Masking tape

1

Draw the design of your choice on the frame of the mirror.

2

Paint a background color on the frame and let it dry.

3

Paint the details, such as the moon and rocket. Let the paint dry before outlining the shapes in black marker.

HINT
To keep from getting paint on the mirror, cover it with masking tape near the edge of the frame.

You can also accent your mirrors with a glitter glue pen.

Beautiful Bandannas

Make your own original and colorful bandannas, decorated in beads, feathers or little mirrors...

Feather Bandanna

1 Sew the feathers along the longest edge of the blue felt.

2 Glue fringe along the longest edge of fabric.

3 Sew a piece of cord at each end to tie on the bandanna.

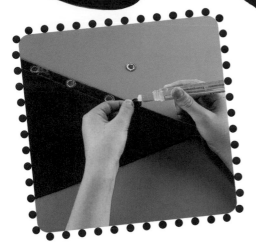

Mirror Bandanna

Glue the pink velvet ribbon to the longest edge of the pink felt triangle. Center the ribbon on the fabric so you have an equal amount of ribbon at the ends. Glue the little mirrors onto the pink ribbon where it is attached to the bandanna.

Madras Bandanna

Trim the edge of the madras with pinking shears so it doesn't fray at the ends. Fold the square into a triangle. Sew beads onto the folded edge that goes around the head. Sew them so the stitches and knots are hidden underneath the fold.

Mail Organizers

These trendy cats will be happy to keep your mail and notes organized.

1

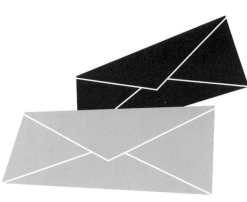

Draw the three parts of your animal on cardboard using the photos as an example. Make the head about 6 inches wide, the middle piece with front legs about 8 inches wide, and the tail end with hind legs about 10 inches wide. Cut them out.

2

Give all the pieces a coat of white paint. Let dry.

3

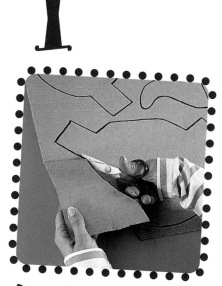

Paint your animal in the colors you choose. You can use one of our models for inspiration.

4

Use a fine paintbrush for small details like the eyes and toes.

5

Cut a cardboard base that is 1 foot long and 6 inches wide. Cut three pieces of cardboard that are 4 inches long by 2 inches wide. Glue the three pieces so they stand upright on the base, near the front, middle, and back. Allow to dry throughout.

6

Paint the base the color of your choice. Glue the three animal pieces to the three upright pieces on the base.

MATERIALS

- Large sheets of corrugated cardboard
- Paint
- Paintbrushes
- All-purpose glue
- Scissors

Floral Picture Frames

MATERIALS

- Corrugated cardboard
- Colored cardboard
- Bristol board
- Wide double-sided adhesive tape
- All-purpose glue
- Artificial flowers
- String
- Ruler
- Pencil
- Nail
- Art knife

Display your favorite picture in this simple cardboard frame. With some creativity, you can turn it into a field of spring flowers!

1

Cut a 12-inch square out of corrugated cardboard and another 12-inch square out of colored cardboard. Trace a 5-inch square window in the middle of the piece of corrugated cardboard. With the help of a grown-up, cut out the window with an art knife.

2

Cover one side of the corrugated cardboard frame with the double-sided adhesive tape.

3

Stick the frame to the colored cardboard. Using the ruler and art knife as shown, cut the colored cardboard in the middle of the frame to make four triangles.

4

Fold back each triangle and use double-sided tape to stick them to the frame.

5

Cut and fold the edges of the colored cardboard and stick them to the frame with double-sided tape. Turn the frame over.

6

Use a nail to pierce holes in the frame. Insert the stems of the flowers through the holes. Place your picture in the frame and tape it at the back. Tape the back of the frame to a sheet of bristol board. Tape a piece of string to the back so you can hang the frame.

Seashell Characters

Make these funny and original characters out of seashells from the beach or craft store.

1 Use modeling clay to fit the two large shells together. Cover the open edges at the back of the shells with clay.

2 Use the modeling clay or glue to stick two shells to the top for the eyes and nose.

3

Use the modeling clay to stick two shells to the bottom for the feet.

4

Cut a piece of wire. Bend two of the wire ends into hands. Stick the wire into the clay holding the body together near the back.

5

Paint the body, eyes and arms in a bright color. When dry, paint a stripe around the edge of the body.

6

Paint the nose red. Paint the feet black, the irises of the eyes white and the pupils black as shown.

Fabric Wall Hangings

Scraps of fabric can be turned into pretty wall hangings to give as gifts.

MATERIALS

- Fabric in an assortment of colors and patterns
- Felt
- Repositionable glue or fabric glue
- Scissors
- Pinking shears
- Fine-tip marker
- Ruler

1 Measure a rectangle 15 inches by 18 inches on a piece of fabric.

2 Cut it out with pinking shears so the ends don't fray.

3

Cut different shapes out of other pieces of fabric. Choose fabrics and colors that look nice together.

HINT
Using this technique, you can create an entire scene out of different fabrics, such as this lovely house.

4

Glue your pieces onto the rectangle. You can layer them to make different designs.

Butterfly Pencil Holder

Collect empty spaghetti boxes to make these pencil holders. You can decorate your wall with them!

MATERIALS

- Empty spaghetti box
- Bristol board
- Mini envelopes
- Colored plastic-covered wire or pipe cleaners
- Small balls
- Paint and paintbrushes
- Scissors
- Glue
- Large, fat nail
- Pens and pencils
- Paper clips

1 Draw the wings on bristol board. Cut them out and paint them.

2 Cut two mini envelopes in half, glue them to the wings, and paint them. Keep open ends of envelopes at top.

3 Cut out a "mouth" into the front and sides of the spaghetti box. Paint the box. Pierce two holes at the top as shown. Curl two pipe cleaners around your finger. Insert the pipe cleaners into the top of the box and glue them in place.

4 Make 12 holes all the way through the sides using the large nail.

5 Cut eyes and pupils out of bristol board. Paint them and glue them on.

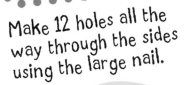

6 Glue the butterfly body onto the wings. Stick paper or foam balls onto the ends of the pipe cleaners and glue them in place.

Artist's Apron

This artist's apron is a practical way to keep clean when you're being creative! Original and eye-catching, you'll want to make more than one to give as gifts to your artistic friends. Here are some designs for you to copy — they're inspired by famous artists like Picasso, Matisse, and Mondrian.

MATERIALS

- White canvas apron
- Felt in assorted colors
- Permanent black marker
- Pencil
- Ruler
- Glue
- Scissors

1 Draw your designs on the apron in pencil.

2 Draw some of the designs shown here on felt.

3 Cut out the felt designs.

4 Arrange them on the apron, and then glue them on.

5 Outline the felt designs in black marker.

6 Add some finishing touches—like drawing dots in black marker along the bottom of the apron, for example.

Surprise Packages

These surprise packages in cheerful summertime colors will brighten up your party. Hide candies, little treats, and surprises inside and give them as party favors to your friends!

MATERIALS

- Colored construction paper
- Colored tissue paper
- Ribbon or pipe cleaners
- Pencil
- Scissors
- Glue
- Adhesive tape

1 Draw a long triangle with two equal 12-inch sides on a sheet of colored construction paper.

2 Cut out the triangle.

160

3

Cut a rectangle out of tissue paper. Make it the same length as the shortest edge of the triangle. Glue it along the short edge. Roll the triangle into a cone. Tape cone so it does not unroll.

4

Cut flowers, stars and hearts out of colored cardboard to decorate the cone.

5

Glue on your decorations. Fill the cone with treats or surprises.

6

Use a ribbon or pipe cleaner to tie up the tissue paper at the top of the cone as shown.

Animal Message Boards

A fish, a crocodile, a cow, a whale... Choose your favorite animal and turn it into a message board. Use the window to write reminders to yourself or funny notes to your family!

Call dad!

MATERIALS

- Large sheet of foam board
- Black construction paper
- Acrylic paint and paintbrushes
- Pencil, white crayon
- Glue, adhesive tape
- String
- Art knife

5

days to vacation!

1

Draw a large oval that is the width of the sheet of foam board. Draw another oval inside, as shown. Draw two lines to mark the front and back of the cow's body. Draw the cow's legs, tail and head on the rest of the foam board.

Buy Milk

2

Ask a grown-up to help you cut out all the pieces using the art knife. Cut out the oval in the center for a window.

3

Paint the cow's muzzle pink. Paint the black spots, hooves, and tip of the tail. Use a fine paintbrush for the rest of the details on the face and ears. Let dry.

4

Glue the legs, tail and head onto the body as shown. Tape a piece of string to the back so you can hang your cow on the door or a wall. Tape a sheet of black paper to the back of the cow so it fills the window. You can turn the sheet around or replace it as needed. Try making the fish, following the same instructions, using white paper instead of black.

Gone fishing!

Felt Key Chains

Carry your favorite animal wherever you go and never lose track of your keys!

MATERIALS

- Felt in assorted colors
- Metal key ring
- Small metal ring
- Leather or plastic laces
- Wooden beads
- Scissors
- Needle
- Embroidery yarn in an assortment of colors
- Cotton batting

1 Cut a heart out of blue felt, a pink circle for the nose, two large brown circles for the head and two small brown triangles for the ears.

2 Cut leather or plastic laces into two long and two short pieces. String a wooden bead on each piece and knot into place at the end.

166

3

Sew on the nose and heart with embroidery yarn. Use small stitches. Sew on some strands of yarn for whiskers. Stitch two small eyes out of black yarn.

4

Stuff a piece of cotton batting between the front and back pieces. Put the ends of the beaded laces and the ears between the two pieces and sew all the edges together.

5

Slip the small metal ring through a stitch near the top and attach the key ring.

GIFT IDEA!
For a birthday or other celebration, these little key chains are so easy to make you can give one to every friend you invite!

Felt-covered Notebooks

For a fun school year, why not cover your notebooks in soft felt? Decorate them with animals to keep you company all day long!

✂ MATERIALS

- Felt in assorted colors
- Scissors
- White glue
- Pencil
- Notebook

1

Cut out a large piece of felt in the same dimensions as your notebook, adding 1 inch extra for flaps to wrap around the sides. Glue the felt onto the cover of your notebook.

2

Fold the flaps and glue them inside the cover.

3

Draw the pieces for your animal on assorted pieces of felt.

4

Cut out each piece of felt.

5

Assemble the pieces to make the animal and then glue it onto the cover.

6

Cut a strip of felt that is 2 inches long and half an inch wide. Glue it onto the cover to hold your pen or pencil.

Girl and Dog Magnets

✂ MATERIALS

MATERIALS

- Foam sheets in pink, orange, brown, cream and black
- Magnetic sheet
- String
- Googly eyes
- Scissors
- Pinking shears
- Glue
- Pencil

Cut out your favorite characters and turn them into magnets for the fridge or locker door!

Draw the pieces you need on the foam sheets, using our models as your guide.

1

2

Carefully cut out all the pieces. Use the pinking sheers to cut the hem of the dress.

3

Glue the head to the hair and the dress. Glue on the bow, eyes, nose, mouth and hearts.

4

Cut four 4-inch pieces of string for the arms and legs, a 5-inch string for the handbag and an 8-inch string for the leash. Glue the strings to the body, handbag and dog. Glue on the hands and shoes.

5

Cut small squares out of the magnetic sheet and glue them behind the head, body, hands, shoes, and handbag.

6

Glue the collar and tongue onto the dog's body. Glue a magnetic square to the back.

Artistic Handbags

Made entirely out of paper and cardboard, these handbags can be given as gifts to your friends, or used to wrap other gifts!

1

Draw the shape of the handbag on bristol board, using our models on the next page as a guide. Cut out two identical pieces for the front and back.

✂ MATERIALS

- Bristol board
- Small paper bag
- Paint
- Paintbrushes
- Pastel crayons
- Glue

2

With the same color, paint the two pieces as well as a paper bag. Before painting, cut the paper bag if it is too tall for your handbag design.

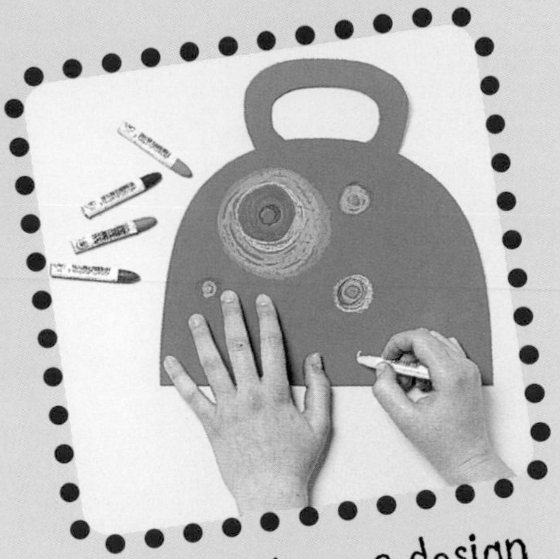

3

Paint or draw a design with pastels on the front of the handbag. You can use one of our models for inspiration.

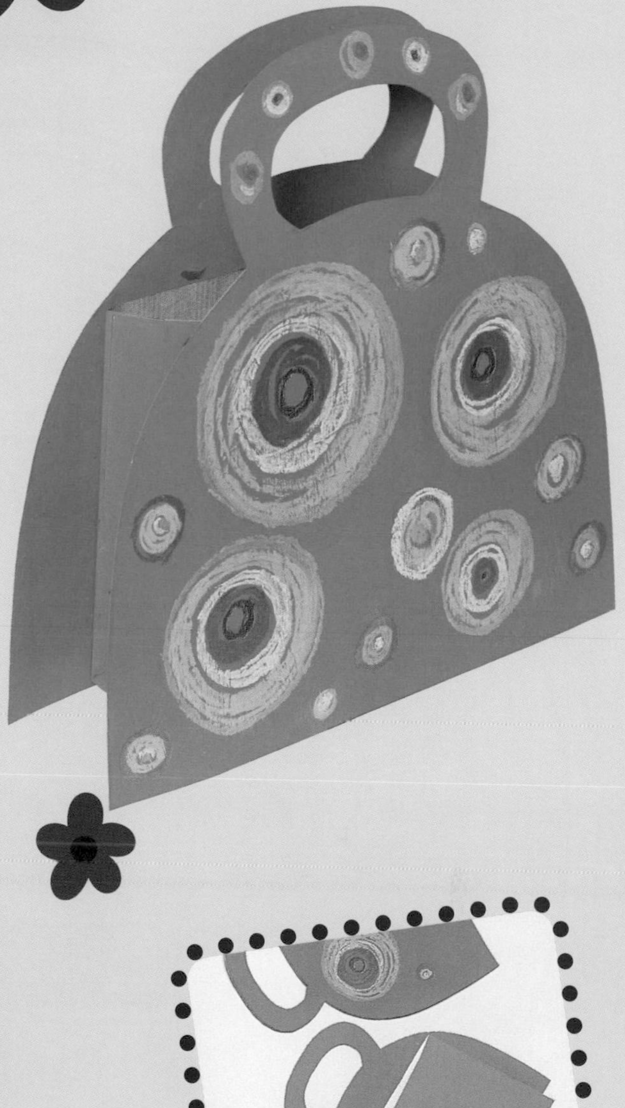

4

Glue the paper bag so it is sandwiched between the front and back pieces of the handbag.

You can enlarge these templates on a copier.

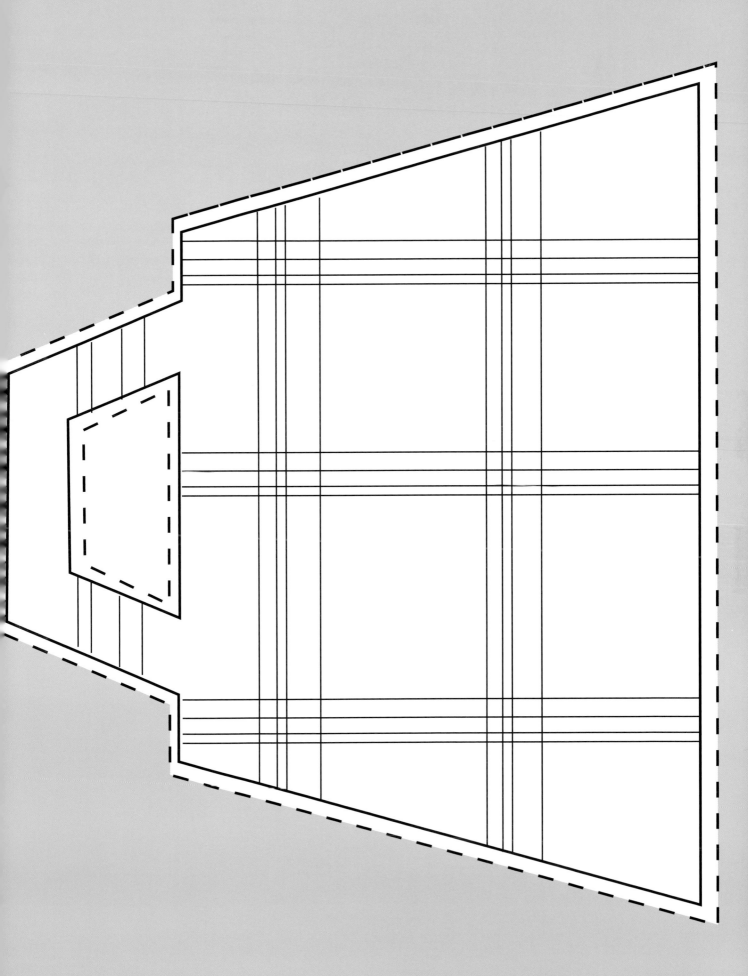

HOLIDAY CRAFTS

HOLIDAY CRAFTS

✂ **MATERIALS**

- Brown corrugated cardboard
- Red, green and dark green corrugated cardboard
- Paper or small foam balls
- Red ribbon
- Gold string
- Green and red paint
- Paintbrushes
- Toothpicks
- Pencil
- Scissors
- Art knife
- Glue

Christmas Wreaths

A holiday wreath on your door sends out warm "season's greetings!" You can welcome friends with two types of homemade wreaths.

1

Draw a 12-inch diameter circle on the brown cardboard. Draw a 6-inch diameter circle inside it. Cut out the larger circle. Ask a grown-up to cut out the smaller circle with the art knife.

2

Paint one side with a thick coat of dark green paint. Let dry.

You can also paint small boxes in holiday colors, tie ribbons around them and attach to the wreath. Follow the example at right.

3

Draw and cut a holly leaf out of cardboard. Use it to trace about 24 leaves in dark green and light green cardboard. Cut them out.

4

Paint the balls red. Stick them onto toothpicks or straight pins to make them easier to paint.

5

Glue the leaves onto the wreath, overlapping them and alternating colors as shown.

6

Glue on the red balls. Cut the red ribbon into 20-inch lengths, tie into bows and glue onto the wreath. Glue a loop of gold string onto the back of the wreath so you can hang it.

Dancing Santa

This cardboard Santa is easy to put together and fun to play with. His arms and legs are moveable so you can make him dance!

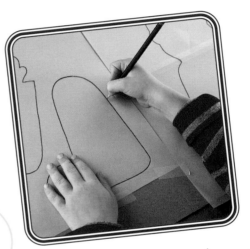

1

Draw the head and body as one piece, and the arms and the legs separately on corrugated cardboard. Cut out the pieces carefully with scissors.

2

Paint the jacket, hat, arms and legs in red. Paint the mittens and face yellow. Let dry.

MATERIALS

- Corrugated cardboard
- Acrylic paint in red, white, yellow, and orange
- Paintbrush
- Pencil
- Fine-tip black marker
- Scissors
- Wooden skewer
- Roundhead paper fasteners

3

4

Paint the stripes on the pants and jacket white, as well as the pom-pom, hat brim, beard and eyes. Paint the buttons and boots black. Let dry.

Fill in the rest of Santa's face in black, red and orange marker or paint as shown.

5

Use the wooden skewer to pierce four holes in the jacket at the shoulders and thighs.

6

Attach the arms and legs to the back of the jacket using the paper fasteners.

Pop-up Easter Cards

Pull the tab and watch the chick pop out of its shell! These cards will make great invitations to your Easter egg hunt!

1

Draw an egg shape on white cardboard. Draw a zigzag through the middle where the egg will split in two.

✂ MATERIALS

- Colored cardboard in blue, green, yellow, red and white
- Pencil
- Glue
- Scissors

2

Cut out the egg shape and the zigzag. Draw and cut out the chick, its beak, and two bunches of grass.

3

Glue the edges of the bottom half of the egg to blue cardboard. Glue on the bunches of grass as shown.

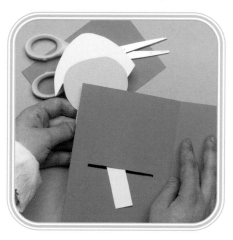

4 Glue the top of the egg to the chick's head. Glue a strip of white cardboard to the back of the chick's head. Make a slit in the back of the blue cardboard behind the bottom of the egg. Slide the strip through the slit as shown.

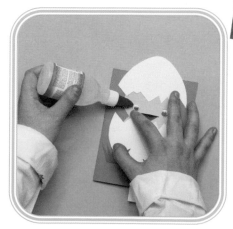

5

Glue on its eyes and beak. Slide the tab in back to make the chick pop out of its shell.

Santa's Reindeer

Santa has nine reindeer to pull his sleigh full of gifts. How many can you make?

MATERIALS

- Foam board
- Foam balls in two sizes (4 larger, 8 smaller)
- Red, green, yellow, orange, and blue crepe paper
- Red, green, yellow, orange and blue paint
- Paintbrushes
- Pencil
- Art knife
- Scissors
- Thin metal wire
- Toothpicks or straight pins
- Twigs

(1) Copy the head, body, feet, neck and tail pieces as shown onto foam board. Have an adult cut the pieces out. Use them to trace three more sets of pieces.

2

Paint the pieces yellow, red, green, orange, and blue as shown.

THE REINDEER GAME

The Reindeer Game is played by two to four players. You will need a dice. Each number in the dice corresponds to a part of the reindeer:

1: Body   4: Neck
2: Front legs   5: Tail
3: Hind legs   6: Head

Each player chooses a different colored reindeer and lays the six pieces flat in front of them. The winner is the first to assemble the reindeer by rolling the dice to get all six numbers.

Egg Faces

Villains, clowns, movie stars... here are characters with plenty of personality! Why not try drawing some unusual faces on your eggs this Easter? These original table decorations are sure to delight your friends.

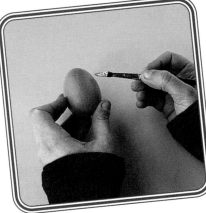

Apply a coat of white paint to the egg and let it dry. Paint color with irregular brushstrokes to give it some texture. Let it dry.

MATERIALS

- Hardboiled or Styrofoam eggs
- Poster paint in assorted colors
- Paintbrushes
- 12 inches of metal wire
- Large spool or small aluminum can

Draw the eyes, mouth, and nose of your character in pencil first.

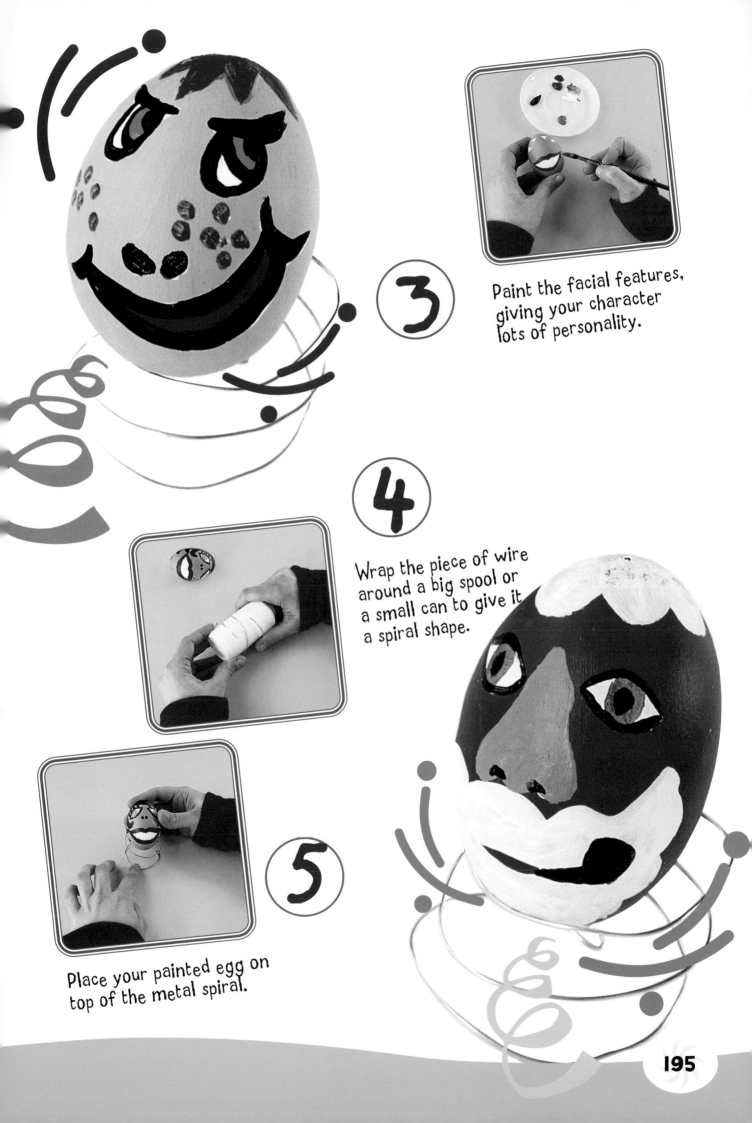

3

Paint the facial features, giving your character lots of personality.

4

Wrap the piece of wire around a big spool or a small can to give it a spiral shape.

5

Place your painted egg on top of the metal spiral.

195

Halloween Puppets

Creepy monster puppets are perfect for Halloween storytelling!

MATERIALS

- Felt sheets in black, blue, purple, and white
- Felt scraps in red and green
- Black marker
- All-purpose glue
- Nail
- Scissors

1

On a separate piece of paper, copy the monster shape so it is large enough to cover your hand. Cut your pattern out. Trace it onto two pieces of felt and cut them out.

2

Glue the pieces edge to edge, except at the bottom, where your hand will go in. Let the glue dry well.

3

Draw, cut out and glue the rest of the features (eyes, hands, teeth, etc.) out of green, red and white felt. Add details with a black marker.

Christmas Tree Gnomes

What funny gnomes! All crooked and quirky—where could they have come from, with their sweet little faces?

Crush the plastic bottle, twisting the bottleneck, to make the body. Position the opening where a nose would be. Cut the large Styrofoam ball in half to make the feet.

Pour a 1/4 cup of acrylic paint into the bottle. Replace cap and shake until the inside is coated. Pour out excess paint and let dry. Then use your paintbrush and yellow acrylic paint on the two halves of the Styrofoam ball.

✂ MATERIALS

- Plastic spring water bottles (ribbed)
- Small foam balls
- Large Styrofoam balls
- Red felt
- Acrylic paint
- Paintbrushes
- Black marker
- Toothpicks
- Glue
- Art knife

3

Apply some glue to two toothpicks, sticking one end of each of them into one of the feet, and the other into the bottom of the bottle.

4

With a marker, draw some eyes onto the small foam balls. To make the hat, cut a triangle out of the felt (10 inches wide by 12 inches long), fold it in half and glue together.

5

Place the hat onto the gnome's head. Glue on the hat and the eyes.

Decorative Candles

Easy to make and beautiful to look at, these decorative candles and lanterns will light up your table for Christmas or Hannukkah.

Sequined Candles

MATERIALS

- Candles in assorted sizes and colors
- Gold thumbtacks
- Sequins, artificial flowers, and leaves
- Beaded straight pins
- Glue

Glue or use straight pins to attach sequins onto a simple candle.

Heart candles

HINT
These crafts are better left unlit. It's safer and you can enjoy them longer.

Trace a heart design in the side of a candle and insert gold thumbtacks or beaded straight pins.

Salt Dough Lanterns

MATERIALS

- Salt dough
- Aluminum foil
- Toothpicks
- Plastic straw,
- Tea light candle with metal holder
- Paint and paintbrush

1

Prepare the salt dough. Flatten it out with a rolling pin on aluminum foil. Cut out Christmas tree shapes or star shapes. Stick a toothpick in the bottom of each tree or star. Punch little holes in them with a plastic straw.

To make salt dough, mix 2 cups of flour and 2 cups of salt with 1 cup of water.

2

Make a round flat dough base for your lantern. Place the metal holder of a tea light candle into the middle of the dough and press down slightly.

3

Stick the Christmas trees or stars into the dough base in a circle. Bake for one hour at 200°F.

After the lantern has cooled, paint it, let it dry, and put the tea light candle into its metal holder.

Chicks on Stilts

Tall and short, striped and spotted, here are some funny chicks to decorate your table at Easter or springtime. Why not make a whole family of them?

(1)

Paint the two Styrofoam balls yellow. Let dry. Attach the balls together by putting a toothpick through the middle of them.

(2) Paint spots or stripes on the chick using a cotton swab.

3 Cut the wings and a triangle for the beak out of bristol board. Paint them.

4 Cut two slits in the body, insert the wings, and glue them in place. Roll the beak into a cone, glue it together, and then glue it to the head.

5 Cut a plastic straw in two for the legs. Make feet out of modeling clay. Insert the straws in them. Let dry. Paint the legs.

6 Make two holes in the bottom of the chick's body using a pencil, insert the straws, and glue them in place. Glue on the eyes.

Festive Placemats

Bring the entire henhouse to the table this Easter. Find inspiration in the color of spring to make these pretty placemats.

✂ MATERIALS

- Burlap (14 inches × 18 inches for each placement)
- Poster board
- Adhesive tape
- Pointy scissors or art knife
- Thick green yarn
- Large needle
- Straight pins
- Acrylic paint in assorted colors
- Paintbrush
- Steam iron

1 Cut a piece of burlap 14 inches wide by 18 inches long. Place a strip of adhesive tape around the edge of the fabric to keep it from fraying.

2 Cut a ½-inch diagonal slit in each corner. Fold each edge inward to make a hem. Use straight pins to hold the fabric in place. Ask a grown-up to iron the fabric to make it flat. Use the green yarn and needle to stitch the hem all around the placemat as shown. Remove the pins.

③ Cut squares out of board for the stencils. Trace your designs on them and cut them out with pointy scissors or an art knife.

④ Place your stencil on the placemat and paint over it. Make sure the paint is dry before you place another stencil close to it or use another color.

MASKS

MASKS

Wild Animal Masks

Have fun making a mask of your favorite animal of the savanna.

MATERIALS

- Paper plates
- Pencil
- Markers
- Yarn
- Scissors
- Glue

1 Paint the paper plate yellow and let it dry. Draw the tiger's eyebrows with a black marker.

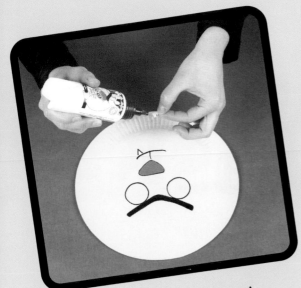

2 Cut a nose out of pink paper and two pointy teeth out of white paper. Draw the eyes and mouth. Glue on the nose and teeth.

3 Draw the tiger's stripes and color them in with brown marker. Glue strands of yarn to the tiger's face for whiskers. Cut out the eyes with scissors.

To hold your mask in place, attach an elastic band to the back of each side of the mask, near the eyes. The bands then go around your ears.

Felt Animal Masks

These colorful animal masks won't frighten off the little ones, and they're easy to make with scraps of felt and paper. Here are a few examples, from a simple teddy bear, to a spotted leopard, to a full-feathered bird.

1

Draw your animal head on a sheet of paper that is the same color as the felt you are going to use.

2

Ask an adult to help you cut out the eyes with an art knife. Cut out the face and the ears with scissors. Lay your paper pattern on the felt, trace the outlines and cut out your felt pieces.

3

Glue the felt onto your paper and press down gently.

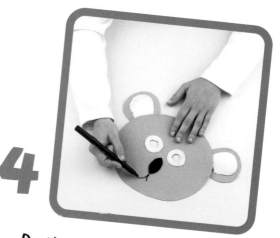

4

Do the same for all the pieces. Glue on the ears and nose. Cut two pieces of ribbon and staple them to the back of the mask at the sides, or attach an elastic band.

HINT
A matching neckpiece will help finish off your costume. You can make one out of paper with felt to match your mask. Add more felt feathers if it's a bird, or draw spots on the felt if it's a leopard.

African Ceremonial Masks

Ceremonial masks, warrior masks, masks for celebrations — African art is rich in abstract design. Using our model for inspiration, make an exotic mask out of cardboard, paper, and glue that is sure to impress your friends.

MATERIALS

- Cardboard
- Paper towel
- Glue
- Pencil
- Paint
- Paintbrushes
- Scissors or art knife

Masks have often figured in traditional African ceremonies and in theater. These kinds of masks would usually be made of clay or wood and decorated in plant fibers.

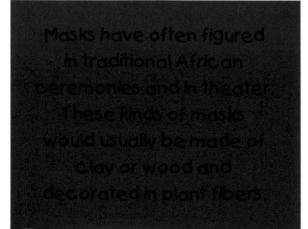

Copy the shape of the mask on cardboard. Draw two large circles in the middle for the eyes.

3 Use the hole punch to make holes all around the top of the cylinder.

4 Using our model as a guide, cut out pieces of red cardboard for the mask's mouth and eyes. Cut out two pieces of black cardboard for the mask's eyes as well.

5 Glue the different pieces to the mask. The mask's eyes should be glued on above your eye holes.

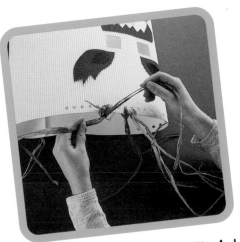

6 Thread strands of raffia into the holes, alternating the colors, and knot them in place.

MATERIALS

- Colored bristol board
- Pencil
- Black marker
- Scissors, art knife
- Glue, sequins
- Feathers
- Elastic thread

Bird Masks

What kind of bird are you? Feathers, glitter, and paper will help you create a mysterious and elegant mask like the kind worn by the actors of the famous commedia dell'arte.

DID YOU KNOW?
During the middle of the 16th century, the commedia dell'arte was a type of theatre based on improvisation. The actors wore masks and performed many acrobatics.

1

Draw the shape of your mask on bristol board. Outline it in black marker.

2

Draw a long triangle out of bristol board. Fold it in half and cut it out.

3

Cut out the mask. Ask a grown-up to cut out the eyes with the art knife.

218

4

Fold back the ends of the nose.

5

Glue the nose to the mask.

6

Decorate your mask by gluing on feathers and sequins.

7

Attach an elastic band to the back of the mask.

Marker Masks

Disguise yourself in this exotic marker mask. All you need is a sheet of paper, a few markers and your artistic talent!

1 Make a grid on the page by tracing a line down the middle of the sheet and then straight across.

2 On the left side of the grid, draw half the mask in pencil.

MATERIALS

- Drawing paper
- Markers
- Pencil
- Ruler
- Art knife
- Elastic band

3

Use the grid to help you draw the right side of the mask so that it is symmetrical to the left. Color in the large areas.

4

Use the black marker to outline the different shapes and to add design details.

5

Cut out the eyes and mouth using the art knife. Attach the elastic band to hold the mask on your face.

Careful! The ink in your markers may run! Start with the lighter colors and then draw the outlines with your black marker.

Paper Wig

With this elegant wig you'd be right at home in a British courtroom...or even the court of a French king! All you need are a lot of white paper and some patience.

✂ **MATERIALS**

- White paper bag
- Sheets of white paper
- Ruler
- Pencil
- Scissors
- Glue

1

Draw the opening for the face on a flattened paper bag.

2

Cut out the opening for the face on the front of the bag.

3

Open the bag.

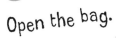

4

Cut white paper into strips 4 inches wide by 10 inches long.

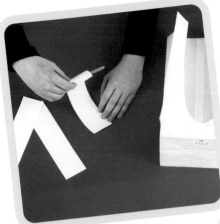

5

Roll the strips of paper around a pencil or your finger to make them curl.

6

Glue the paper curls onto the bag one by one. Start at the sides.

7

Alternate the direction of the curls and don't make the rows too straight. This will give the wig more volume.

Indonesian Masks

Papier-mâché is often used to make dolls and headdresses in Asia.

GLUE SOLUTION
You can make glue solution by combining four parts white glue and one part water.

1 Inflate a balloon and lay it on a table. Hold it in place with masking tape. Tear sheets of newspaper into narrow strips.

2 Dip strips of newspaper in glue solution and apply them to half of the balloon in crisscrossing layers. Let each layer dry well. Roll strips of newspaper dipped in glue and apply them to the head to form the eyes, mouth and eyebrows. Let dry.

3 Apply a thick layer of white paint over the mask. Let dry.

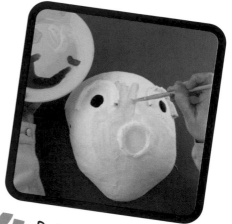

You may find inspiration in photographs of traditional feasts in Asia and Indonesia.

4 Paint the base color of the mask.

5 Paint the rest of the details of the face with a fine paintbrush, highlighting the eyes, mouth, nose and cheeks in different colors.

225

Bat Mask

Create a mask that sorcerers and witches will love!

MATERIALS

- Violet, white, light green, and black poster paint
- Paintbrushes
- Bristol board 24 inches x 8 inches
- Stapler
- 12-inch length of elastic
- Stapler

Using our model as a guide, draw the bat on bristol board.

Carefully cut out the bat.

Paint the bat's wings violet and the eyelids light green. Paint the pupils and the rims of the eyes black. Pierce two holes in the pupils for your eyes.

2

3

4

Pierce two holes where you will pass the elastic through, then knot it in place.

HINT
Proceed the same way
to make a cauldron or
pumpkin mask!

Collage Masks

Cut photos of animals, fruits, or plants out of magazines and make outrageous collage masks reminiscent of the style of Italian artist Guiseppe Arcimboldo.

Cut a large face out of a magazine. This will be the base of your mask. Draw a curved line on the face so that the mouth and jaw are below the line. Cut off the lower part of the face.

2 Cut photos of your favorite objects in different sizes and colors out of a magazine or catalog.

3 Glue the mask onto the sheet of paper. Arrange the animals above the eyes and glue them on in layers.

4 Cut off the extra paper at the top of the mask.

5 Cut out the eyes in the mask. Pierce a hole on each side of the mask, pass the ends of the elastic band through the holes and knot them in place.

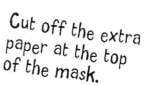

Handyman's Mask

Surprise your friends with these original masks. Even though they're made out of cardboard, they look like you hammered them together out of wood and metal!

MATERIALS

- Corrugated cardboard
- Brown paper
- Kraft paper
- Black and gold markers
- Art knife and scissors
- Glue and tape
- String

1 Cut a rectangle the size of your face out of corrugated cardboard. Draw two squares of different sizes for the eyes. Cut them out with an art knife or ask a grown-up to do it.

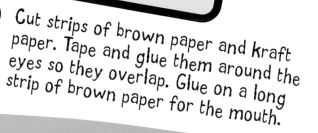

2 Cut strips of brown paper and kraft paper. Tape and glue them around the eyes so they overlap. Glue on a long strip of brown paper for the mouth.

HINT

You can make a costume to go with your mask. Find a large cardboard box and paint it gray to look like metal. Draw circles on it to look like bolts.

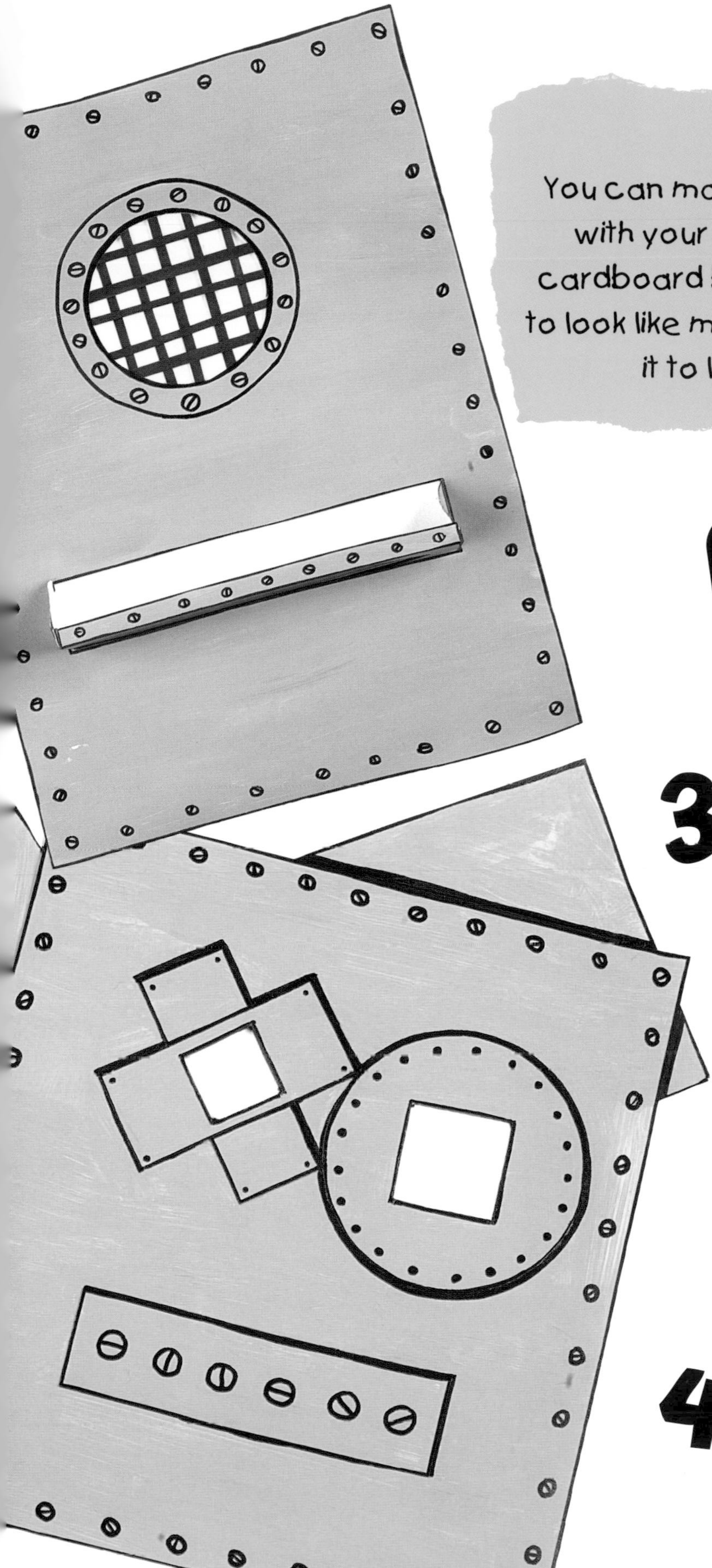

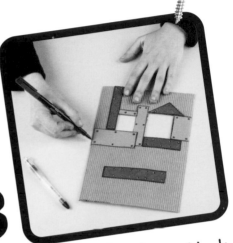

3

Outline each strip in black marker, then draw black circles near the edges to look like screws. Add a spot of gold to each black circle.

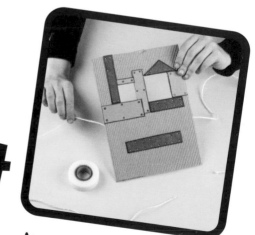

4

Attach a string on each side of the mask, at the height of the ears. Why not try making other masks, using these models for inspiration?

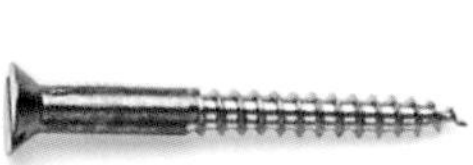

WORLD CRAFTS

Malian Headdresses

Conjuring up all kinds of animals, these headdresses are inspired by a tribe in Mali. Traditionally worn during important celebrations, these headdresses may honor the rain or appeal to nature for a plentiful harvest.

MATERIALS

- Large sheet of brown cardboard
- Stapler
- Hole punch
- All-purpose glue
- Scissors
- Brown raffia

1 Cut a strip of cardboard. It should be 7 inches wide and long enough to fit around your head with 1 inch extra to overlap. Use the hole punch to make holes near the base that are 1 inch apart.

2 Using these photos for inspiration, draw the different pieces for the headdress on the cardboard.

For a headdress that stands up, use sturdy paper and make sure the shapes you cut out are at least an inch wide.

3
Cut out the pieces, assemble them and glue them together.

4
Staple the strip of cardboard so it fits around your head. Make two 3-inch cuts in the top, one above each ear.

5
Thread strands of raffia through each hole near the base, tying knots in them as you go along.

6
Insert the main piece of the headdress into the two cuts so that it stands up.

DID YOU KNOW?
Traditional African dances have their roots in rituals linked to the economic and social life of a community. There are dances for fertility, marriage, harvest, hunting, and war, among many others.

Seashell Mask

In the Democratic Republic of the Congo, it is traditional to make masks decorated with seashells. With this one for inspiration, why not make your own? Instead of seashells, you can use bits of cereal or dry beans that look like the real thing!

MATERIALS

- Bristol board
- Poster paint: blue, red, green, white, ochre, brown
- Puffed wheat cereal or dry beans
- Scissors
- Pencil
- Paper glue

1 Draw the shape of the mask, and then the eyes, mouth, nose, and eyebrows.

2 Cut out the mask as well as the facial details. Save all the pieces.

3 Paint each part of the mask with poster paint.

4 Glue the facial details back onto the mask, bending them first so they stand out from the face.

5 Glue bits of cereal or beans onto the hat and face in a geometric pattern.

Dragon Puppets

Have fun making these colorful dragons, and then watch them come to life in your hands! Why not put on a show with your friends — and make the puppets dance.

MATERIALS

- Square box
- Styrofoam balls, large and small
- Paint in assorted colors
- Paintbrushes
- Glue
- Paper streamers
- Red and white lightweight felt
- Art knife
- Scissors
- Glue stick

DID YOU KNOW?
In China, dragons symbolize the Emperor. The dragon also represents heavenly and creative power, as well as authority to the Chinese.

1

Cut the square box on three sides only and fold it.

2

Apply an undercoat of white paint over the entire box. Allow it to dry.

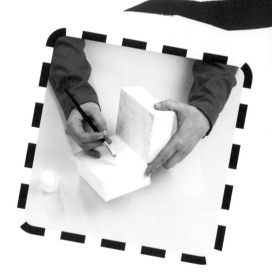

3

Paint the box black inside, and another color outside.

4

Cut the streamers into long strips of different sizes to make the puppet's tail.

5

Cut the large Styrofoam ball in half to make the eyes, and then paint the pupils black.

6

Glue the streamers to the box using the glue stick.

7

Glue on the eyes. Cut out the teeth and a long tongue from the felt. Glue them on.

8

Paint the small Styrofoam ball red and glue it on for the nose.

Boomerang and Shield

The Aborigines of Australia carved boomerangs and shields out of wood. You can make your own out of cardboard, using traditional designs to give them an authentic look.

MATERIALS

- Bristol board in warm colors like red and ochre
- Pencil
- Markers
- Scissors
- Poster paint
- Paintbrush

1

Draw the boomerang on bristol board with a pencil. Outline it in brown marker.

Cut out the
boomerang
with scissors.

Using our model as a
guide, draw a traditional
design on the boomerang
in brown marker.

Don't use too many different
colors, and always stay in the
warm range. White paint adds
contrast and makes the
design stand out more.

Add white paint
to the design.

Add yellow
or brown to
the design.

Babila and the Sorcerer

Storytelling is a celebrated tradition throughout Africa. Songs, poems, and stories have been carried down year after year through the spoken word. Perhaps, you will make up some stories about Babila and the Sorcerer and their "Little African Village."

Pieces for the Sorcerer

1

Cut the feet and arms out of brown paper. Form a cone with the yellow construction paper and glue it together with the glue stick. Use the template as a guide.

2

Cut a small rectangle of yellow paper and glue it into a larger rectangle of brown paper. Cut the edges of the brown paper to make it jagged.

3

Draw the details of the sorcerer's mask as well as the designs for his robe using a marker. Glue the mask to the top of the cone. Glue the arms to the back of the cone and glue the feet inside the cone. Bend the feet so the cone stands upright.

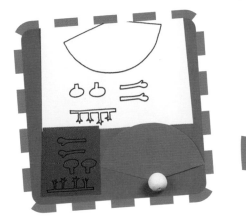

4

Do the same for the Babila character, but cut a circle for the head and paint it brown.

Pieces for Babila

Little African Village

This little village sets the perfect scene for many stories starring Babila and the Sorcerer.

MATERIALS

- Construction paper
- Thin wood, twigs, or straw
- Kraft paper
- Glue stick
- Scissors
- Markers
- Paint

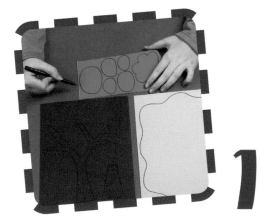

1

Copy the different shapes on colored paper and cut them out. Use brown paper for the tree and its base, green for the leaves, orange for the flames, and light brown for the roof of the house.

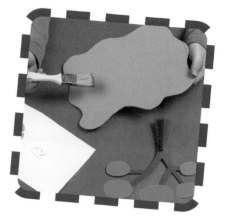

2 Cut the shape of the ground out of cardboard and paint yellow. Glue the leaves of the tree onto the branches. Make a slit in the trunk and in the base to fit them together. This cross-shape will help the tree stand up.

3

Make a cone-shaped roof out of the kraft paper, glue it together and cut a fringe around the edge with the scissors. Cut the house out of corrugated cardboard, glue it into a cylinder shape and place the roof on top.

Cut three pieces of balsa wood—two small and one larger. Consider breaking a twig instead or cutting a straw into three pieces. Glue the two small pieces to either side of the larger piece to make a cross. Fold the flames at the base to make a tab and glue them to the balsa wood cross.

4

Egyptian Frescoes

Paint a scene from everyday life in the land of the pharaohs. These scenes appear on the frescoes that decorated the tombs of the ancient kings and queens. Choose the kinds of colors that were used on the frescoes, like ochre, brown, blue and white. These resemble natural pigments that came from the earth and rocks.

MATERIALS

- Construction paper
- Glue stick
- Scissors
- Markers

1

Looking at pictures of Egyptian frescoes for inspiration, draw your designs in black marker, filling in all the spaces on your paper. Our model shows pillars decorated with vegetables, animals, and a hunter with a bow and arrow.

A word of advice: Draw your characters in profile, and keep your shapes simple.

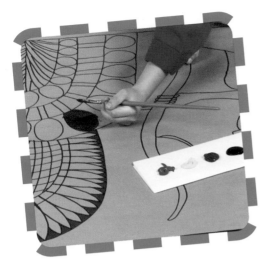

Think of other scenes from daily life in ancient Egypt, like fishermen in a rowboat on the Nile, dancers, or servants bringing offerings to the pharaoh.

2 Paint the designs, choosing harmonizing colors. Let the paint dry well.

3

Use the black marker to outline the designs again, if necessary. This will make them stand out.

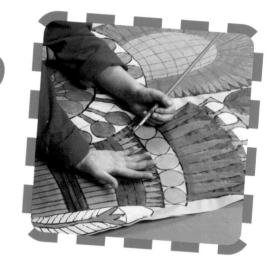

269

Tatooed Hands

In this traditional craft, the artist's own hand becomes the canvas! Imagine a variety of exotic designs for the palms and the fingers! Hang these decorated hands on your bedroom wall. They are also a pretty way to display your rings and bracelets!

1
Trace your hand on the sheet of bristol board with a marker.

2
Cut out the hand.

3 Paint it a solid color and let it dry.

4 Draw decorative patterns with the pencil and then paint complementary colors over them with a fine paintbrush.